Lesser Known
Weymouth

Lesser Known
Weymouth

Julie Musk

When we lay where Budmouth Beach is,
O, the girls were fresh as peaches,
With their tall and tossing figures and their eyes of blue and brown!
And our hearts would ache with longing
As we paced from our sing-songing,
With a smart Clink! Clink! Up the Esplanade and down.

(*The Dynasts*, Thomas Hardy)

Roving
Press

Published by Roving Press Ltd
4 Southover Cottages, Frampton, Dorset, DT2 9NQ, UK
Tel: +44 (0)1300 321531
www.rovingpress.co.uk

First published 2012 by Roving Press Ltd

ISBN: 978-1-906651-107

British Library Cataloguing in Publication Data
A catalogue record for this book is available from the British Library

Photographs and maps by Roving Press unless stated otherwise.
Cover design by Tim Musk
Frontispiece photo: beach near Stone Pier

Set in 11.5/13 pt Minion by Beamreach (www.beamreachuk.co.uk)
Printed and bound by Beamreach (www.beamreachuk.co.uk)

Contents

Preface

Lesser Known Weymouth is the second in a series of *Lesser Known* guide books which look at specific places in some detail – rather like having your own local guide to show you around and point out the interesting bits.

Weymouth today comprises Melcombe Regis, together with the villages of Nottington, Broadwey, Preston, Radipole, Upwey and Wyke Regis, which until 1933 locally governed themselves and had their own parish councils. Nowadays, all these different areas comprise Weymouth. For reasons of space, this book concentrates on the area of old Weymouth and Melcombe Regis and only mentions these outlying villages in passing.

This is not a detailed history book, as the town's past is covered in many other excellent titles. However, the past is so much tied with Weymouth's development that I can't help bringing it in, but hopefully with a 'lesser known' twist. Essentially the book is a contemporary look at Weymouth, highlighting local people, businesses and organisations that are unique or special to the area. Apologies to anyone who feels they were left out.

Stories and anecdotes are usually more interesting than facts, and this book hopes, above all, to be a good story. Local people are the best source of such material, and their narrative is interspersed with background details and personal observations. Hopefully you will discover some lesser-known facts and places from reading this book and will use it to explore. With this in mind, at the back of the book are six walks, with quiz questions to keep younger readers interested. Enjoy!

Julie Musk

Acknowledgements

Thanks to everyone who contributed or helped in any way with the book, in particular Ray Banham, Ann Tate, Alan Rogers and all the individuals who took the time to give me their personal stories and check the text. Thanks also to Dave Allan and Brian Jackson for reading and commenting on the history sections.

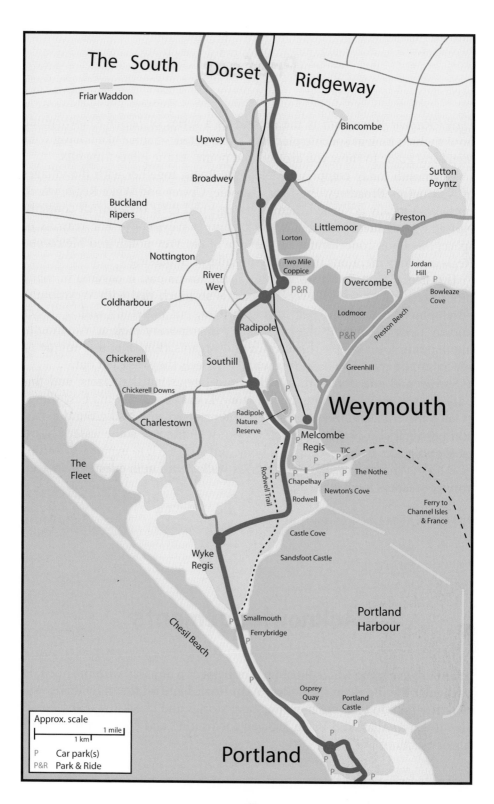

Introduction

Weymouth has had its fair share of excitement over the years – ransacking by French pirates, its own inhabitants at loggerheads over the harbour trade, the Black Death decimating the population, Civil War, bombing by Germans (Weymouth was one of the most heavily bombed towns in the country) and troop billeting by thousands of Americans.

Other towns were quite envious of Weymouth and Melcombe Regis having two MPs each to represent them. Over the years, the citizens of the two towns have been represented in Parliament by some distinguished names. In 1584 Sir Francis Bacon (pioneer of the scientific method) was MP for Melcombe. Sir Christopher Wren represented Weymouth in 1702. Sir Thomas Fowell Buxton was MP for Weymouth in 1818. He is famous for, among other things, helping to abolish slavery and is commemorated on the back of our £5 note. His family home was Belfield House in Belfield Park Avenue, off Buxton Road: '… said to have been a surprise gift for his wife, who outlived him by

The octagonal Spa House in Nottington was built c 1830 over the spring and has a central column inside containing the well. It comprised a pump room, two bathrooms, a dressing room, two sitting rooms and six chambers. Its local nickname is Sixpenny-Bit House/Thre'-Penny Cottage. On the gate piers next door sit two stone pelicans.

many years and made this gracious house the visiting place of George III and his family during their frequent Weymouth sojourns' (Ricketts 1975, p.25).

If it hadn't been for its medicinal waters, Weymouth might have developed very differently. There were two sulphur springs at Nottington and Radipole and another naturally clear spring at Upwey. The benefits of Nottington's water were first enjoyed by a sheep, which fell into the water and was cured of scab. The observant shepherd then drove his whole flock in for a bath and cured all. 'The virtues of this water in all cutaneous and scorbutic complaints are astonishing. It has performed such cures as if generally known, would immortalise its fame!' (John Love, larger than life local public figure, late 1700s). It is believed King George III used to drink from the Wishing Well at Upwey using a special gold cup, a replica of which is presented annually at Ascot Races. Such medicinal springs together with the perceived benefits of seawater bathing made Weymouth popular, besides its pretty seaside location.

The town's popularity as a resort and spa really got going when the Georgian Royal family came to enjoy the health-giving benefits of the waters and fine sandy beach. Indeed, Weymouth's sands are said to be the best for sandcastle-making in the south, and the young Royals would have had a splendid time on the beach while their father was wheeled out to sea in his bathing hut. As forms of transport improved, hordes of grockles (tourists) arrived by paddle steamer and later by train from London, Bristol and Bath. In 1937 the Spanish-style Art Deco Riviera Hotel at Bowleaze Cove attracted the more affluent car owners due to its exclusive location, and in 1939 the new Pier Bandstand opened, *the* venue for wrestling, beauty contests, dancing and roller skating. Osmington PGL Centre on the eastern hillside overlooking

Jordan Hill and Bowleaze Cove, with the old Riviera Hotel in the distance. The building bankrupted its first owner, was a Pontins holiday camp in the late 1950s and is now privately owned. Grade II Listed, it is a prominent feature along Weymouth Bay.

Weymouth started as an adult-only camp, described in 1972 as 'the place to whoop it up' and 'the swing camp of the south'.

If you think Weymouth is overcrowded and has traffic problems today, just look back to the 1950s. Photographs in Maureen Attwooll's *Weymouth: The Golden Years* show horrendous traffic jams and parking problems, the beach packed with families. Congestion around the King's Statue was so bad that some people were calling for the Statue to be moved, some even questioning why keep it at all. Eventually the site was made into a large roundabout and George got to stay put.

Things have moved on apace since then. The following statistics (source Dorset County Council, November 2010) are revealing:

- 26% of households in Weymouth and Portland do not have a car – the lowest level of car ownership in the country.
- Average house prices are lower than national and county averages (£189,108 compared with £242,103 across Dorset and £219,832 across England and Wales).
- Four areas in the borough have been identified as amongst the 20% most educationally deprived in England.
- 25% of the population of the borough is over retirement age.
- 6.5% are Black or Minority Ethnic (nationally the proportion is 13.2%).
- Socio-economic classifications show a much more even distribution between the five top-level categories than other parts of Dorset. Just over 28% are 'comfortably off', 21% are 'wealthy achievers' (compared with an average of 43% across Dorset) and almost 41% are either of 'moderate means' or 'hard pressed', significantly higher than the county average (18%).
- The unemployment rate is 3.1% – the highest of the six Dorset districts.
- The average weekly wage of Weymouth and Portland residents is below the national average.
- The rate of crimes involving violence is high at 22.5 per 1000 residents – compare this with the rate for Dorset (10.1) and nationally (17.0).

An Observation

Despite this, much hard work and regeneration has taken place with the run-up to the 2012 Sailing Olympics. As Councillor Ray Banham observes:

'… 20 years of redevelopment completed in just over 24 months! We are fortunate to have been given a great opportunity to start building a future – not only for local people, but also for the growing younger generation. Haven't you noticed how we are blessed with our young staying and working in their "home town", whereas in other seaside locations they are filling with residential homes? Nothing

against that, I'm old myself, but what future do these locations have? Most will remain stale and "old fashioned", and what good is that? Our borough is vibrant and alive. Weymouth and Portland have always been a location well worth a visit, with year-round events and entertainment to suit the whole family, plus the bonus of a beach second to none, a safe haven for families to enjoy, and once visited and discovered, to return time and time again to. We want to give out the message "Come to Weymouth and Portland, you are very welcome".

So why is Weymouth doing so well, when others are suffering? It has always fared well, and progressed much the same as others, but in recent years an opportunity arose which at the time seemed like doom and gloom. When the Royal Navy and naval air station left Portland port, this resulted in the loss of hundreds of jobs and in the dockyard going on the market. Several bidders came forward, but one of them promised a future of redevelopment, jobs, plus the security of maintaining the protective sea wall – this company was Portland Port. On securing the dockyard, work began on the clearance of old buildings, with new units built in their place. Slowly different companies are renting these and bringing back all the employment that had been lost, gradually becoming once again a thriving area. While this was going on, Granby Industrial Estate also was expanding. New companies were investing in the area, with the retail park opening, and part of the main town centre being bulldozed to make way for a new shopping precinct, which was opened in 2000. A time capsule was buried at the same time with different artefacts chosen by schools in the borough (my idea).

In 2003 the Yachting Association had the opportunity to build a new sailing academy at Portland Port, but to secure the finance for such a large project it had to obtain £1 million from Weymouth and Portland Council. At that time, money was rather restricted. At a full council meeting, I argued that with the forthcoming bids for the Olympics, it could mean the difference between our county being successful with its bid. The financial implications were vast; it was a small investment for a possible financial bonanza. It was a close thing, but following my speech it was agreed to make the investment. Since then, major investment has taken place. The Sailing Academy has been thriving, with world championships taking place and Olympic sailors from all over the world coming to get used to the area, the tides, wind, etc., plus they have invested in properties and spent their money in the area's shops and restaurants. The bypass has been completed, with new park-and-ride facilities. The whole Esplanade has been regenerated, with new street lighting, uplighters for the refurbished shelters, the King's Statue completely restored, the Jubilee Clock also, and to top it all, a new laser lighting attraction shining out to sea. A lot of pavement areas have been widened, to expand the "café culture" being encouraged in the town, and the icing on the cake is a new Esplanade surface. The Pavilion complex also is showing signs of prosperity, whereas 2 years ago there were threats to it even being there.'

Ray's positive outlook is refreshing and it is good to see the area thriving. The legacy of the Olympic Games includes the 7.2-km (4.5-mile)-long Weymouth Relief Road, opened in 2011 after 60 years of waiting, at a cost of £89 million, and the Weymouth and Portland National Sailing Academy, which was the first venue completed for the Games, opened by the Princess Royal in 2005.

Weymouth is a great place for a night out, day visit or holiday, and the large number of pubs (67 at last count according to *West Dorset Pub Guide*) is due to the fact that a third of the town's economy depends on tourism, followed by sailing and fishing. With revamping of key areas, Weymouth looks set to continue to attract visitors *and* be a great place to live.

The Past

Weymouth has a long, illustrious past which needs to be understood before you can really explore and appreciate the town and its environs.

Bronze Age stone axes and swords have been found in Radipole Lake, church scrapers and knives on the Fleet, and Neolithic burial pits on the Ridgeway; during this time there would have been hundreds of round barrows on this ridge and some have been discovered quite close to the centre of town, including one at Redlands, where skeletons and fragments of arrows have been unearthed. Weymouth Museum has a section of mosaic flooring from a Roman villa discovered in Newberry Road, Chapelhay. Roman galleys used to sail up the river as far as Radipole, where they unloaded their cargo for transporting over the Ridgeway to Durnovaria (Dorchester). Radipole is one of the oldest parts of the borough, lying on both banks of the River Wey, where remains have been found of a Roman port and village, and a burial site was unearthed near the top of Spa Road.

On Jordan Hill to the east of town are remains of a Romano-Celtic temple. The site was excavated in the 19th century and again in 1931, when archaeologists found a well-like pit beneath one corner of the sanctuary wall approx. 13 ft deep. At the bottom was a stone cist containing two urns, a sword and spear head. Pits like this were used for ritual offerings by the Celts. More than 80 skeletons were found in a cemetery north of here, buried with grave goods (bowls, brooches and spoons) which are now on display in Dorset County Museum. A separate hoard of more than 4000 Roman coins was also found on the hill summit. An old Roman road runs over Gould's Hill at Upwey straight to Maiden Castle, linking Dorchester with the Roman harbour base. The old Dorchester to Weymouth road (A354) constructed in

Jordan Hill Roman Temple probably dates back to the 4th century AD. It is situated off Bowleaze Coveway tucked away among houses, and is looked after by English Heritage.

1824 broadly followed this, with its hairpin bend designed to cope with the steep gradient; now the relief road takes travellers away from this ancient route. Broadwey village grew up along this Roman road and took its name from the fact that the River Wey broadens here.

The first written recordings of Weymouth are from Saxon times. In AD 934 King Athelstan gave much of the area to Milton Abbey, and there was a lot of feuding at this time. Wyke Regis is far older than Weymouth. It has an ancient centre with medieval buildings, which the Wyke Regis Protection Society is proud to maintain, and Norman All Saints Church. The churchyard is full of shipwreck victims, as Portland wouldn't take 'Kimberlins' (outsiders). Wordsworth's brother John lies in an unmarked grave, having lost his life along with 250 others when the ship he was on (the *Earl of Abergavenny*) ran aground on the Shambles and sank in the bay. There were so many bodies requiring burial, they were even laid to rest inside the church, filling almost the entire floor. Jean Bellamy writes in *101 Churches in Dorset* (2006):

'An unusual feature of this church is a room containing an irregular hagioscope [squint] and known as the "Bones Room". Now used as a vestry, its somewhat gruesome title derives from post-Reformation days when it was used as a depository for bones which came to the surface during the digging of graves in the churchyard. This was a not infrequent occurrence, for normal internments were limited to the south side of the church, the north side (once known as the Devil's Side), being reserved for outlaws, criminals and suicides, as well as having close associations with shipwrecks and smugglers. The resultant overcrowding of the south side led to some unavoidable disturbance, particularly as medieval graves were not more than 3 ft in depth. In 1870 the collection of bones in the Bones Room was buried in a large grave dug opposite the old rectory.'

Another church with an interesting history is St Ann's in Radipole, built in 1815 on the site of a much older church (St Mary's). This pretty church, dwarfed by old yews which vie for space in its crowded cemetery, is full of European architecture and looks and feels Pre-Reformation. A painting by Sir James Thornhill graces the altar, religious scenes by local artist Ann

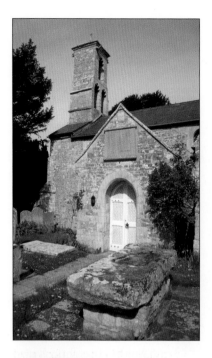

Tout adorn the ceiling, and the blue and white-painted pews are decorated with wildflowers. A Victorian gallery looks down on the whole scene, replacing an earlier musicians' gallery. The tidal estuary used to extend to the foot of the hill below the church before Westham Bridge (constructed in 1921) effectively dammed the water flow. St Ann's is remote from the village centre today. Once trade opened up with France, the southern (Weymouth) side of the river was first to be settled by people from Wyke mooring their boats there, while Radipole men carried on using their lake-head village.

To the right of the door of St Ann's Church is an ancient Druid altar. Superstitious foreign travellers might have prayed to their gods here on first arriving in such a strange place.

St Ann's churchyard has some lovely carved headstones. Obscured by undergrowth in a far corner are some commemorating those drowned aboard the Earl of Abergavenny.

Weymouth was said to be founded in 1244, Melcombe in 1268. Weymouth originally occupied a constricted site, hemmed in by the harbour and Portland Bay. Melcombe, built on a small spur of land between the sea and a saltwater marsh on reclaimed ground, was much better situated and developed unrestricted, with a regular grid of streets, which still survive in the old part of town today with the two high streets of St Thomas and St Mary. According to *Kelly's Directory of Dorsetshire 1898*, Melcombe takes its name from an old mill that once existed here. Before 1280, the Abbot of Cerne owned much of the local area and he gave Melcombe to Edward I, whence it became known as Melcombe Regis. The borough had two MPs, along with neighbouring Weymouth. Half the river and thus half the harbour trade belonged to each town, and by the 14th century both towns had grown considerably and were vying for the trade in wool exports. There were disputes over harbour rights and dues paid by docking ships, robbing and scuttling of rival merchant ships, their MPs constantly at each other's throats and causing a nuisance in Parliament: 'Between [these towns] arose a great controversy, both enjoying like privileges, and both challenging the particular immunities of the haven, which lyeth in the very bosom of them' (*The Beauties of England and Wales*, 1803).

In 1346 during the siege of Calais, Weymouth provided 20 ships, compared with only four from Poole, indicative of how much larger Weymouth was then. However, a few years later came the Black Death. The plague first entered the country through the port at Melcombe as flea-ridden rats carrying deadly bacteria jumped ship. It proceeded to infect and kill up to 50% of the population in just 2 years. After being bitten by a flea, victims began to exhibit flu-like symptoms, followed by painful black boils in the groin and armpits, swollen lymph nodes, internal bleeding, fever, delirium and raging headaches, leading to death. The disease 'started under the armpits and spread across Europe', according to Sir John Verney (noted wit and author). It is little wonder the two boroughs went into drastic decline. As the disease gradually subsided, the townspeople began to rebuild their lives, scraping a living from the quays and warehouses that served the shipping trade.

In the 15th century the two towns were decreed official ports of embarkation for pilgrims travelling to Spain, together with Dartmouth. Vessels overladen with pilgrims left the harbour regularly. Weymouth was still a one-street town in those days (the old High Street running behind the fire station, along the quayside, down Trinity Road and into Trinity Street), restricted by salt marshes, with a steep hill rising 80 stone steps to the Chapel of St Nicholas. Both boroughs were at this time losing out to growing Poole, and the continued squabbling didn't help matters. Tired of the situation, Elizabeth I passed a Charter in 1571 amalgamating the two boroughs under one name of Weymouth (as recognition of the location of the original river settlement). But alas, it made little difference to the inhabitants. In 1594 the first Town

Bridge was built in an attempt to bring the two sides together, with limited success.

In 1625, aided by Reverend John White, the tall-ship *Abigail* left Weymouth with pilgrims bound for the New World. Reverend White was a kindly man, known as 'the Patriarch of Dorchester' for his charity and godliness. (He is laid to rest in St Peter's Church in Dorchester, commemorated by a brass plate in the porch.) Besides the Reverend's spiritual motive, he had a practical consideration for forming a colony in the New World. Weymouth fishermen had to brave 3000 miles of Atlantic Ocean to fish the cod banks off New England and Newfoundland, and a friendly land base would provide them with much needed shelter and provisions. The pilgrims settled in Wessagusset, New England. Devon man John Endicott sailed from Weymouth in 1628 to become the first governor of Massachusetts. Unlike White, Endicott had 'the reputation of being a narrow-minded bigot who banned merriment and deviation of any kind' (Dwyer 2009). Robert Gorges, a soldier-sailor from Bradpole near Bridport, established a settlement north of Massachusetts, which he named Weymouth, thereby founding the state of Maine.

Then came English Civil War in 1642. Parliamentarians were in charge of the town, but a group of Royalists very nearly succeeded in taking over. Attacking Royalists from Weymouth and Portland bombarded their Parliamentarian neighbours in Melcombe Regis during the Great Battle and Siege of Weymouth, which lasted 19 days. Nine hundred Parliamentarians held out against 4500 Royalists. A cannonball can still be seen in the gable of a house on the corner of Maiden Street and St Edmund Street. The town suffered much, being made a garrison and possessed variously by both sides. The First Civil War ended in 1646 with the Parliamentarians winning, and the last Royalist castle in Dorset surrendered in April 1646 to Admiral Batten and the Parliamentarian-controlled Navy.

In 1751 the tax on spirits was increased in an effort to curb drunkenness among the common people. This led to a rise in smuggling along most of the south coast. Also in the mid-1700s something happened to take the focus away from the harbourside feuds. Doctors began advocating saltwater bathing as a cure for all manner of things (gout, rheumatism, skin complaints, gunshot wounds, bruises, strains, eye problems, etc.); it was even recommended as a cure for 'persons of corpulent habits, who become unwieldly' (according to local author John Love, himself obese). As visitors started to arrive, intent on enjoying the healthy benefits of the sea, the seafront was smartened up and the harbour improved. Imports arrived to meet the needs of the growing town, and trade with the Channel Islands took off. In particular, potatoes, flowers and tomatoes were imported from the Channel Islands, with grain, fertiliser and building materials exported.

Ralph Allen was an influential socialite at the time, and when he fell ill his doctors advised the 'saltwater cure'. So he took himself off to Weymouth, where his health improved. In 1780, the Duke of Gloucester (King George III's younger brother) came to Melcombe on Allen's recommendation to try 'the cure', which worked so well he took up summer residence. Then came the King himself. His Family is said to have holidayed almost every summer in Weymouth from 1789–1805, originally staying at his brother's Gloucester Lodge. Thus gradually Weymouth was transformed from a commercial port into a fashionable resort – 'England's Bay of Naples'.

In 1794 the Post Office chose Weymouth as the main base for a regular service to the Channel Islands. Weymouth offered the shorter distance compared to rival Southampton and, being nearer to Falmouth, could link with the ocean mails. Weymouth's mail packets were single-masted cutter rigs, speedy craft in a favourable wind and capable of reaching Guernsey in 12 hours, although 20–30 hours was more usual. Often they carried more smuggled spirits than passengers. Admiralty cruisers kept an eye on the packets, providing relative protection from French pirates. The Postmaster General issued a warning to passengers, who often experienced insults from rough captains who were deemed 'exceedingly gross and violent persons'.

Steam power was introduced in 1827 for the Post Office packets running to the Channel Islands, which proved faster and more reliable. This service ceased in 1845. In the same year, the paddle steamer *Rose* started offering a regular service from Southampton to Weymouth, but this ceased in 1847 with the extension of the railway from Southampton to Dorchester. Cosens & Co. paddle steamers are very much tied with the development of Weymouth,

The world's last sea-going steamer, the Waverley still calls into the Stone Pier, offering day cruises for up to 900 passengers along the Jurassic Coast in September. She was built in 1947 and restored to her original condition with a grant from the Heritage Lottery Fund.

and for 119 years their vessels provided the main form of transportation to holiday resorts up and down the coast. They also served as liberty boats when the Navy was in the bay, as salvage vessels and as tugs for visiting sailing ships.

Trains first arrived in Weymouth in 1857. In those days, rail travel was affordable, with cheap excursions popular with the working classes, bringing visitors from London, Bristol and Bath.

- Upwey Wishing Well Halt – situated above the hairpin bend opened 1905 for visitors to alight and enjoy the waters of the well. The old steps that led down to street level can still be seen adjacent to the present road bridge.
- Upwey Junction – opened April 1886, replacing the original Upwey station in Old Station Road which had opened in 1871. The new station served the Abbotsbury branch that had opened the previous November. Renamed Upwey and Broadwey following closure of the Abbotsbury branch in November 1952, it became unstaffed in March 1965 and was refurbished during 1987. The Friends of Upwey Station keep it tidy and in good order.

'There is not much that I can do,
For I've no money that's quite my own!'
Spoke up the pitying child –
A little boy with a violin
At the station before the train came in –
'But I can play my fiddle to you,
And a nice one 'tis, and good in tone!'
The man in the handcuffs smiled;
The constable looked, and he smiled, too,
As the fiddle began to twang;
And the man in the handcuffs suddenly sang
Uproariously:
'This life so free
Is the thing for me!'
And the constable smiled, and said no word,
As if unconscious of what he heard;
And so they went on till the train came in –
The convict, and boy with the violin.

(*At the Railway Station, Upway*, Thomas Hardy)

- Radipole Halt – opened 1905.
- Weymouth Shed – had a 60-ft turntable installed in 1925.

- Quay Tramway – the Weymouth Harbour Tramway running along Commercial Road from Weymouth station opened in October 1865 for goods traffic. At first the wagons were drawn by horses, until June 1880 when a small steam locomotive was used. The first passenger trains ran over the tramway in August 1889 when the Great Western Railway took over the vessels of the Weymouth & Channel Islands Steam Packet Company and commenced boat trains to and from Paddington in connection with sailings. Freight traffic ceased in 1972, with the regular boat trains following in 1987.
- Weymouth to Portland line – opened October 1865.
- 'Admiralty' or Breakwater line – 1 mile (1.6 km) long, used mainly to haul coal to the breakwater, opened 1878.

Regular cargoes of clay, coal and agricultural exports also went through Weymouth port. In the 1870s potatoes were an important revenue earner, with on average 12,000 tons a season imported. Special Jersey potato boats and trains ran twice a week, helping to offset losses made on the passenger steamers. Imports of French broccoli and Guernsey tomatoes similarly waxed and waned; Jersey flowers are now usually air-freighted.

In 1860 the French invasion threat prompted construction of the Solent forts and Portsmouth and Portland Harbour defences. The first breakwaters were built between 1849 and 1872 to shelter the Royal Navy and provide safe anchorage. The breakwater was constructed using local Portland stone, mainly by the inmates of Portland jail, and the black-and-white Chequered Fort was armed with fourteen 12.5-inch guns.

Robert Whitehead designed the first practical torpedo in 1866 for the Austrian Navy. The British Navy could not buy foreign-made equipment so Whitehead started a factory at Ferrybridge in the 1890s and at *HMS Vernon* at Bincleaves to manufacture British-made torpedoes, which proved very effective later in WWII against Russian submarines. As well as his factory, he developed the area, providing housing and schools for his workers. The building of a pier allowed the launch of torpedoes into Portland Harbour even at low spring tide, and its base timbers can still be seen at very low tide. A railway took torpedoes and men to the end of the pier, where torpedoes were placed in boats and taken out to the firing platform in the harbour. The factory ceased production in 1963 and the site is now covered with 'Harbour Point' homes, but the old rail-track bed is still there in the cycleway/footpath of Rodwell Trail. A modest foundation stone can be found at the end of Whitehead Drive (seen easily from the Trail). As a small aside, Whitehead's grand-daughter married the Austrian Von Trapp of *The Sound of Music* fame.

Another notable accomplishment took place in 1912, when a Short S38 'amphibian' (hydroplane) took off from the warship *HMS Hibernia* while she was travelling at 5 knots across the bay. The biplane safely landed at Lodmoor airfield, a major achievement in the history of aviation. In 1913 motor racing used to take place on the beach, with cars reaching nearly 60 mph close to the water's edge. The names Cobham Drive and Stainforth Close bear witness to two famous aviators of the time. Sir Alan Cobham was knighted for his pioneering flights in 1926 between London and Australia. He flew all round Britain offering flights in his DH61 Giant Moth and his display team (Cobham's Flying Circus) visited Chickerell three times to wow spectators. Sir Alan believed, 'It is vital to the safety of the nation that Britain should become a nation of aviators'. He was also Director of Airspeed (a company that built airplanes). In 1931, former Weymouth Secondary School pupil Flt Lt George Hedley Stainforth AFC RAF broke the air speed record by flying in excess of 400 mph in his Supermarine S.6B aircraft. This feat is commemorated by the Stainforth weather vane in Greenhill Gardens and by the prestigious Stainforth Trophy, awarded annually by the Air Officer Commander-in-Chief RAF Strike Command to the operational station within the Command that has produced the best overall performance.

During WWII, Weymouth Bay was declared a defence area, the beach covered with barbed wire and closed to the public, and the harbour could only be used by the Navy. Because of its gentle slope, the beach was an ideal testing ground for amphibious military craft. Billeted soldiers arrived and

many of the resort's main buildings were taken over, including the Royal Hotel, which became the US military's HQ, and the old Riviera Hotel at Bowleaze Cove, which became a home for disabled evacuee children. Six thousand evacuees came to Weymouth and the town was a focal point for troop movements. Nothe Fort has photos of American GIs enjoying coffee and doughnuts before setting off to Normandy for D-Day. Local packet boats were used as mine sweepers due to their shallow draft and also brought wounded soldiers back from Dunkirk. Americans built the car park at Chesil Beach as part of their D-Day preparations.

The cenotaph on the Esplanade opposite the Royal Hotel was unveiled in December 1947 in memory of the part played by American servicemen during WWII.

Relative to its size, Weymouth was one of the most heavily bombed towns in Britain. By the end of the war, after 51 air raids, 83 people had been killed and 7417 properties damaged (Dwyer 2009). Pomeroy (2005) states that 4300 incendiaries, 481 high explosives, 9 oil and 4 land mine bombs were dropped on the town. This is partly explained by the fact that Chesil Beach was a bombing range and Chickerell and Lodmoor had airfields – prime targets – not to mention the Navy presence in the harbour.

As well as being a bombing range, the Fleet was used to test Barnes Wallis's bouncing bombs. These were designed to spin and skip across water, jumping torpedo nets, dipping underwater, then at the right depth taking out the side and bottom of an enemy ship or of course the famous German dams. Mounted in a Wellington bomber, these spherical-shaped bombs were backspun by a chain drive and dropped on Chesil Bank, with the target normally the waters of the Fleet. In trials they managed up to 22 bounces. RAF Chesil Bank Bombing Ranges officially closed in 1959. RAF Chickerell also closed in 1959 and the site was redeveloped for housing and light industry (as Granby Industrial Estate).

The first German submarine was relinquished to the Royal Navy at Weymouth. Rear-Admiral Scott received the declaration of surrender and commented, 'It seems appropriate to me that the first U-Boat to surrender after the war should do so at Weymouth, the spiritual home of the Royal Navy's Anti-Submarine Service'. An air station (RNAS Portland) was built in 1917 as a seaplane base, the aircraft operating from the base's slipways until aviation operations ceased in 1919. Then, in 1946, Hoverfly R-4Bs moved in and the base became a heliport, formally commissioned as *HMS Osprey* in 1959. A short runway and landing spots were built to take Wasp, Wessex and Lynx aircraft, and at one time the slipway was used by hovercraft. The air station closed in 1999 and was redeveloped with a maritime flavour, as a base for Sunseeker and the Sailing Academy. HM Coastguard Search and Rescue helicopters still use the heliport.

In 1997 the UK's one and only prison ship (*HMS Weare*) was moored in Portland Harbour. She closed in 2006 after conditions on board were criticised by the Chief Inspector for Prisoners, and later departed for Nigeria to be used as accommodation for oil workers.

There have been several plans to reactivate the old town tramway since its closure to regular traffic in the early 1980s. In 2007 Jurassic Coast Railways Ltd, in conjunction with city business associates and an internationally renowned UK-based civil engineering group, began working on multi-million pound proposals to provide a heavy rail link from the main-line railway station at Weymouth to Easton on Portland using around 75% of the former railway trackbed, which closed in the mid-1960s. This would have enabled a direct connection to Osprey Quay, the significant development plans of Portland Port (a new 'super berth' for 'world class' cruise ships) and other major property and infrastructure proposals. At about the same time, JCR Ltd was in discussion with a major UK property developer, Howard Holdings Ltd, who had won a competitive process to redevelop the 10-acre (4-ha) Pavilion site at the end of the tramway where the Channel Island ferries operated from. Their £150 million-plus plans included a marina, hotel complex, luxury flats, retail and leisure facilities and a rebuilt theatre. Howard Holdings proposed a significant 'developer contribution' towards reactivation of the old tramway which would have an 'end on connection' with the Portland rail proposals. The scheme would utilise the latest technology including low floor, hybrid trams which do not need overhead power lines and have almost zero carbon footprint. At Weymouth station there would be a tram stop link and footbridge to a new two-deck car park over the existing Radipole car park for an additional 1000 cars. The tram would act as a shuttle to the new Pavilion site, taking cars off the narrow local streets to help solve some of the chronic traffic congestion.

As a second phase of the tramway development, a new route was proposed to link the holiday camps and residential areas in Preston, along the seafront to the Pavilion and the phase-one tramway and thus through town to the railway station. However, despite the work being well thought through and supported, the main driver was the planned development of the Pavilion site, which stalled due to political and mainly economic factors, and has meant that plans have been shelved for the foreseeable future. This is much regretted by some as the project would have created major regeneration and employment and a flagship 'signature' site to promote Weymouth. The tramway is now formally no longer part of the national rail network, and the local council wanted to rip up the old rails which they considered a safety issue. However, the cost of doing so would be prohibitive so for the time being it is staying.

Securing the bid to stage the 2012 Sailing Olympics has focused much attention on Weymouth and Portland and left a legacy for the future. Today the town has a vibrant new identity, with a great mix of marine and leisure industries and many annual events showcasing the area's strong maritime heritage.

The Harbour and Sea

Fishing

Commercial Fishing

Commercial fishing from Weymouth centres on shellfish (brown crab, spider crab, lobster), whelking and wet fish. The *Nicola L* moored near Hope Square is one of the larger scallop and mussel boats. Brown crab are sold worldwide, but 'Portland crab' commands a premium for its high quality, and the area has a long-standing reputation for crabbing. It is possible to catch right up to the shore, although there are rules regulating the type of boats that can fish that close in. Kim Scard, partner of long-time Weymouth fisherman Paul Lynham, explains:

> 'The rule is that any boat more than 12 m long cannot fish within 6 miles (9.7 km) of the coast. This stops the huge trawlers coming too close in, protects the habitat and preserves the stocks. We regularly catch juvenile crabs and return them – it's encouraging to see there's been no decline in the stock. Like most sea creatures, crabs are nomadic, they move around according to season, so that's where the fisherman's experience comes in, knowing where they are likely to be. Paul has been involved in a crab-tagging exercise with a sample batch of crabs. Fishermen catching the tagged crabs were asked to send the tags back to record how much the crabs had grown, how long they'd escaped recapture, how far they'd travelled; it was surprising how far they'd gone. It's the not knowing/speculating that makes fishing exciting; also the bits of wreckage and strange creatures that we drag up – it adds a sense of wonderment.
>
> We fish every day, weather permitting. Big spring (high) tides preclude the boat going out. The tide chart is our bible, the weather our fate. Paul stakes out the traps on areas of the seabed – there's a gentlemen's agreement between fishermen so that everyone is allowed some space to lay pots, and certain types of boat, e.g. bottom draggers, keep out of this area. The gear is marked so you can tell who's who. Boats head out at first light and come back around 4–6 pm, the crews working 12-hour days. The majority are day fishermen, though some stay out all night and some visiting boats are out for several weeks before returning to port. On a good day during peak season we might catch up to 1 tonne of brown crab and up to 100 kilo of lobster. Most of our catch goes to Portland Shellfish Ltd via holding tanks at S&W Shellfish Ltd on Portland. It's good to see businesses in the same industry thriving in the same area. People think that the price of crab sandwiches is high, but if they realised what effort went into catching and processing them they'd understand. That's why I try to spread the word by giving talks and slide shows about the fishing to local groups and school children, and show them how to cook and dress crabs. It's a protracted exercise from sea to plate.'

The local commercial fishing fleet comprises mostly boats less than 12 m long. Most fishermen specialise in one type of catch, though some double up according to season.

The fish landing area on Custom House Quay complies with EC regulations concerning the landing of fish for human consumption, and harbourside electrical sockets mean that modern lorries can keep their refrigeration generators going without running their engines. Fishermen are free to choose where and how they sell their catch. Some sell direct to local outlets and markets, many through local agents Weyfish on Weymouth Quay or S&W Shellfish Ltd in Chiswell, Portland. The catch is weighed on the landing area and taken to S&W's depot which has live holding facilities. Crabs are cooked on the premises and the meat extracted, packed and sold to customers, including top restaurants in London. Some live crab and lobster are sent to Billingsgate Market for onward distribution to London wholesalers or export to Spain and France.

Whelks follow the cold water, so winter is the busiest time for whelk fishermen. They are caught using crab bait, bagged on the boats and brought back to the landing area for weighing. A lorry from a factory in Kings Lyn collects and takes them for cooking and exporting to places like Korea, at the rate of approx. 20 tonnes of meat per month.

Angling

There are several good local spots which don't require any special permission to fish from:

- Stone Pier (under the Nothe): float fishing using mackerel and ragworm as bait. In summer: wrasse, mackerel, pollock; winter: dog fish, whiting.

- Pleasure Pier (behind the Pavilion): in spring/summer: plaice, dab.
- Chesil Beach: good all-year-round fishing. The cod season is Nov to end of Feb. In spring: plaice, dab, flounder; March–Nov: smooth-hounds (mini shark), ray, bream, triggerfish, dog-fish, bass. The Portland end is good for conger eel.
- The Fleet lagoon: you cannot fish from a boat, only spin from the shore with artificial bait (no live bait). The Fleet is a bass nursery and it's a legal requirement to return any fish less than 45 cm long.
- Preston Beach: in spring/summer: mackerel; winter: bass.
- Bowleaze Cove: spinning for pollock, bass, mackerel.
- Harbour: mullet in summer, eels in winter.

Radipole Lake is classed as river fishing; no night fishing is allowed and you must have a licence and buy a day ticket to fish off the decks here (available from Reels & Deals in St Thomas Street and the Weymouth Angling Centre in St Edmund Street). Nev works in the Weymouth Angling Centre:

'We're open from 6.30 am till 6 pm every day and people arrive early in the morning to get their bait, etc. before going out for the day. We stock all kinds of frozen bait – squid, sand eel, mackerel, mussels, razorfish, black lugworm, cuttlefish, hermit crab, and pike packs for river anglers. Also live ragworm and peeler crabs. We do special deals on mackerel fishing – combo rod, reel and tackle – and other deals all year. The shop sells everything you need, including crab lines. You can crab anywhere in the harbour. We sell a lot of preserved bait to kids who don't like handling live worms!'

Owner Andy Selby organises competitions for local fishermen (see in-shop posters). He runs a flat fish competition every April and a cod open in November, as well as charter-boat competitions. He also supports *MV Freedom*, a local charter boat run by volunteers as a charity. The boat is specially adapted for wheelchairs, to give people with disabilities and learning difficulties and the elderly the freedom of the open sea.

The Weymouth Angling Centre also sponsors the local junior section of the Weymouth Angling Society – a family-friendly club with premises on Commercial Road on the inner harbour. The Club's Inter-Schools Junior and Summer Angling Competitions are popular, and they also hold monthly shore and boat competitions and have leagues for ladies and juniors. The club offers temporary membership to visitors and their families. Junior anglers are especially welcome and are given guidance on not just how to catch fish and what tackle to use but also the correct way to handle fish and their speedy release if not required for the pot. The club has a healthy social agenda with darts, pool, whist and cribbage, social functions, and race, auction and bingo nights. Its club house is available to other local groups to use for meetings, being in a prime spot by the marina.

Sailing and Boating

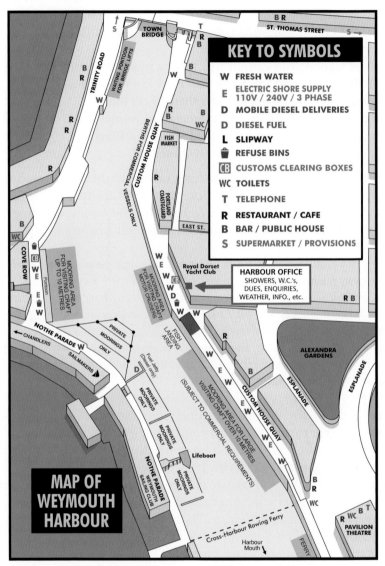

Berthing map (courtesy of Weymouth and Portland Borough Council).

Weymouth is the closest port on mainland England to Cherbourg (66 miles/106 km), St Malo (125 miles/201 km) and the Channel Islands (54 miles/87 km). The harbour offers a safe port in times of strong south-west winds, when boats can wait it out before venturing out round Portland Bill. Portland Race is a dangerous tide race and rocky underwater ledges add to the confusion of waters here. Coastwatch has information on sea conditions around the Bill.

Weymouth Harbour is popular with yachtsmen, being sheltered and easily accessible and offering alongside berthing. With a plethora of drinking places and restaurants, Weymouth attracts 1000 or so resident craft and around 6000 visiting vessels each year. The Harbour Master's website has helpful information for first-time visitors and a local community page. The traffic light system atop a mast on the south pier guides shipping in this busy harbour, with Condor Ferries slipping in and out of the melée, barely raising a wash. At times, swarms of small boats head out, intent on winning local fishing competitions. Before entering the outer harbour, visiting vessels should contact the Harbour Master for berthing instructions. Visiting yachts over 12 m are usually directed to Custom House Quay, vessels 10–12 m to the north side and smaller craft to the south ('the Cove' in front of Cove Row). Sheltered Newton's Cove has a rocky landing. Portland Harbour comes under a separate authority and if you go inside the breakwater there is a charge. The Harbour Master's launch boat is on the water during summer and errant or speeding craft are called to order by loudhailer, much to the amusement of onlookers.

The bridge lifts generally on the hour every 2 hours (first lift is at 0800) and in summer boats simply queue up and wait; at other times it is necessary to request a lift (allowing 1 hour's notice). The times have been carefully worked out in conjunction with bus schedules and the emergency services. There is a waiting pontoon just below the Bridge on the port side and Channel 12 has announcements of lifting times.

The inner harbour has two marinas. The council-owned marina provides competitively priced moorings with over 400 berths. Facilities include fresh water and electricity available at most berths. The private-run Weymouth Marina on Commercial Road is a stylish, purpose-built marina with more than 300 berths including visitors' berths. Being minutes from the town centre, train station, beach and restaurants, and with no tidal restrictions, it is very popular and there is usually a waiting list to keep a boat here. Boats arriving in the old harbour should call the Marina Office, which is staffed 365 days a year. The Marina provides electronic pontoon gates, 24-hour CCTV and a private car park. All berths are supplied with electricity and fresh water, and there are private washrooms, laundry facilities and WiFi broadband. Neil behind the desk explains how the Marina is run:

'Before the marina was built in 1998, there was an old wall – you can still see the stakes of this at low water – and the area was silted up. Dean & Reddyhoff dredged it and then constructed the marina. People from as far away as the Midlands keep their boats here, as the south coast is the best for sailing; about 40% travel over a hundred miles. We have mostly pleasure craft – 40% yachts, 60% motorboats – no commercial boats (to keep things looking nice). We get lots of characters and over the years some celebrities have kept boats here. The Spirit Yacht of James Bond/Casino Royal fame used to be berthed here, and Round Britain and Ireland Challenge boats are also based here. We have a very small tide – just 2.5 m, compared with the Severn Estuary which has 14.5 m. The only restriction to coming and going is the Town Bridge.'

Modern facilities, a choice of berths and a great location within walking distance of town mean that Weymouth's marina is suited to all types of boat users and craft.

You may launch a boat from the Slipway in the inner harbour, accessed from Commercial Road, and from Bowleaze Cove. Windsurfers and kayakers can launch from Overcombe Corner. A permit is required for any powered aquaplaning activity in the bay, including jet-skiing, waterskiing, wakeboarding and the towing of ringos, etc. Anchorage does not require permission and the southern end of the beach is popular, being sheltered, easily accessible and handy for town.

The area between Bincleaves and Smallmouth attracts a lot of dinghy sailors, windsurfers and bathers. Moorings here belong to various local sailing, yacht and cruising clubs. Venturing inshore of these moorings runs the risk of a boat getting stuck on the underwater ledges. It is possible to land on Castle Cove Beach; the pier here is owned by the sailing club but they welcome visitors. You can also land to the east of Western Ledges between Castle Cove and the breakwater. There is another beach west of Sandsfoot Castle at the end of Old Castle Road. Ferrybridge Boatyard has a slipway and chandlery open to all. During Portland Speed Week on 'The Ham' at Smallmouth (known as Sailboard Alley) windsurfers vie for space. The smooth water and increased wind here are ideal for them.

The old entrance to the Fleet is now a small harbour owned by Ilchester Estate. Most sailing boats cannot get under Smallmouth Bridge and powered vessels are restricted. Where the Fleet becomes shallower, only rowing boats are permitted. Check the tides before exploring this lovely area from the water.

The concrete slip and small pier at Bowleaze Cove are mainly used by jet skiers, who have a designated area here. Under Furzy Cliff is a submerged wall of Portland stone, protecting the cliffs from erosion. This wall runs parallel to the shore as far as the flats at Overcombe. Orange buoys in summer mark the western end.

Alistair Hampson is a local sailor: 'I crew on a 28-ft W-class yacht and we take part in Weymouth Sailing Club race meetings during summer (Monday and Thursday evenings). The thrill of competing in the lovely and relatively sheltered Weymouth Bay is sometimes enhanced by spotting the odd dolphin pod.'

The Sailing Academy, Osprey Quay

According to the Olympic Sailing Committee, Weymouth and Portland Harbours have the best sailing water for small boats in northern Europe, with their combination of clean winds, sheltered waters and weak tides. No wonder then that the area was chosen to host the 2012 Sailing Olympics. After significant marine civil engineering works involving reclaiming part of the harbour, building new slipways, pontoons, berths and work to the breakwater, the Weymouth and Portland National Sailing Academy (WPNSA) opened in 2005 on the former RNAS site. Facilities include:

- A 150-m-wide slipway accessible in all states of wind and tide
- Three cranes for hoisting yachts
- Parking for 600 dinghies
- 125 protected berths for ribs and yachts

- On-site dinghy sailing, yachting and windsurfing schools (run by third-party operators)
- Full on-water event support
- Campervan site for visitors.

Among the high-profile events taking place here are the UK Windsurfing National Championships, Sigma 38 and J109 yacht racing, Sail for Gold, Laser World and National Championships, the International Federation for Disabled Sailing (IFDS) World Cup, Contender World Championships (dubbed the world's most popular single-handed trapeze sailing dinghy) and RS All Classes Regatta (a fun competition involving a range of different race courses). The Academy also hosts multi-sports such as Big Bay Swimming, triathlons and rowing. Round Britain and Ireland Challenge (RBIC) yachts use the Academy as a training ground, it being the start and finish port.

Local charity the Chesil Trust offers 'Sail for a Fiver', a scheme for local school children aged 10–11 to try sailing for half a day at minimal cost. The programme is part of the Academy's philosophy of helping less-privileged children try water sports and supporting them through to racing events. As a not-for-profit company, the WPNSA maintains close contact with the local community. Another way is through its Volunteer Programme. No previous marine-based experience? No matter. Anyone may apply to learn and gain globally recognised qualifications and foundation skills at the Academy, especially appropriate for those looking to start a career in the marine and events industries.

The Royal Dorset Yacht Club (RDYC), Custom House Quay

The RDYC welcomes all visiting mariners to enjoy the hospitality of its club and its stunning view over the harbour. The Club has royal connections going back to 1875 when the Prince of Wales (later George V) was an active member, sailing in many races aboard the yacht *Britannia*, and her burgee and racing flag are proudly displayed on the wall upstairs. HRH Duke of Edinburgh keeps up the royal patronage today. Outside, along the Quay, are shower and toilet facilities and noticeboards displaying weather forecasts, tide tables, useful telephone numbers, Bridge opening times and minimum landing sizes of fish and shellfish. 'Victuals 2 Go' is popular with boaters whereby the Club's chef can provide certain items (favourites like curry and lasagna) from the menu, ready frozen for simple reheating on board.

Weymouth Sailing Club, Nothe Parade

Weymouth Sailing Club has moorings for about 100 boats, a dinghy park, slipway and crane. It caters for IRC cruisers, fast and slow cruisers, and dinghies, including Squibs – a class of two-person dinghy popular in Weymouth, which has the largest national fleet at approximately 30 boats. The club has a busy racing schedule, and two members are national champions. Races are held on Monday and Thursday evenings. There is a promising youth section known as YOBs (Youths on Boats), and those lacking sailing experience can join and crew for others. Sir Robin Knox Johnston (the first to sail single-handed non-stop around the world) visited to record a programme for *Radio Solent* and declared it was one of the friendliest clubs he had ever been to. Enthusiastic Squib sailor Alan McDine explains why Weymouth is such a popular place to sail:

'For one thing there's very little commercial traffic compared with the Solent, where craft are crossing in all directions and racing there is a bit of a lottery. Also we have fairly consistent winds and a small tide. The only real challenges are the currents that sweep around the bay – you have to know if they're coming or going – and you get some difficult winds under Nothe Fort and against the breakwater. Also getting in and out of the harbour without an engine can be a bit of a challenge. You soon see who the sailors are then!'

Weymouth and Portland Cruising Association (WPCA)

WPCA is a friendly and informal sailing/motor boat club for those who enjoy cruising or just messing about in boats. Racing is not normally a feature of its activities. With no premises of their own, members of the Club meet at the RDYC every Tuesday from 7.30 pm. They organise trips to local anchorages for BBQs and gatherings as well as further afield, talks (often by members about their cruising exploits), visits, social events and an extensive summer cruising programme. Their fleet comprises nearly 80 different boats, and they welcome new members and anyone new to boating. One benefit of membership is use of a number of swinging moorings in Portland Harbour which are allocated on a first-come first-served basis. Telephone 01305 776488 for more details.

Diving

As one of the largest manmade harbours in the world, the sheltered waters of Portland Harbour offer year-round diving opportunities, making it a popular destination for scuba divers at all levels. A fleet of professional local dive boats in Weymouth and Portland offer day trips and charters to the majority of the inshore and offshore wrecks in the area.

There are more wrecks per square mile in the English Channel than anywhere else in the world and several wrecks are found just off Weymouth and Chesil Beach as well as within Portland Harbour itself. A 19th-century paddle steamer, *The Countess of Erne*, lies inside the northeast arm of the breakwater, making it a popular dive at a maximum depth of 17 m. Other good dives are the 1900 Spanish steamship *Enecuri*, a barge, a dredger, a landing craft and even an experimental WWII 'Bombardon Unit'. Other popular wrecks outside the harbour lying in the waters of the Channel include the *Salsette*, a P&O liner; the *M2*, a virtually intact submarine; and the *Aeolian Sky*, still with much of her cargo strewn over the seabed.

The archaeological site of the *Earl of Abergavenny* is one of dozens of wrecks with historical importance outside Weymouth Harbour lying underwater on the shores of nearby Chesil Beach. The *Earl* was part of a small fleet of East Indiamen on route from Portsmouth to Bengal and then onto China. She hit the Shambles, was freed by her crew, then made her way to Weymouth but sank before reaching safety. She lies about 2 miles (3.2 km) off Weymouth Beach.

The Weymouth and Portland Sub-Aqua Club, like all BSAC clubs, is primarily for local divers and individuals interested in the sport (http://sites.google.com/site/weysac/). Its 'try dives' are for anyone who wants to give diving a go; this typically involves a brief poolside introduction to the equipment and techniques, followed by a scuba dive in the pool. They have a wide range of equipment in various sizes available for students/members to hire, a compressor and club boat. The latter is available to all suitably qualified members, can carry up to ten divers and is fully equipped. Members meet at the Angling Society clubhouse on Thursday nights.

Various local companies offer a full diving package. Underwater Explorers is a diving centre and school in Portland offering recreational and technical diving courses at all levels. Their website www.underwaterexplorers.co.uk has useful local information (tides, weather, dive sites, etc.). Scimitar Diving runs three boats from the harbour to local and offshore sites throughout the year. Their website www.scimitardiving.co.uk has updated dive boat schedules and local air and gas fill prices. The main local guide book is *Dive Dorset* by John and Vicky Hinchcliff.

Lifeboat Station

John Harvey was the last Commanding Officer of the air station at Portland and is now Operations Manager of the Lifeboat Station. From his window overlooking the station, he has an excellent view of the goings-on in the harbour. As we were chatting, three guys in a small sailing boat were trying to dock at the Lifeboat pontoon; they were obviously uncertain how to go about it and were having some difficulty. John commented with some amusement, 'It's one way to learn! I'll just keep an eye on them in case they need help.' He explains how the Weymouth Lifeboat Station works:

'The coxswain and mechanic are the only paid members of the crew, the rest of us are volunteers. I support the cox one week in four as the duty launcher and act as link between the Coast Guard and Lifeboat crew; when there's an emergency, I page whoever's on call and make up the team. We have quite a few call-outs for missing divers, which we nearly always find. The usual problem is they come up too quickly and get the bends. It doesn't help if they've been drinking the night before! We also rescue yachtsmen whose engines won't start or who get stuck when the wind drops, although we aren't a towing service. Visiting sailors who don't know the area often get into difficulty in the Race and send out a mayday, but left to their own devices they usually come through unaided, spat out the other end by the tide. There's a steady stream of fishing boats with problems, and drifting inflatables. Also some suicides. In the Fleet we use a small black inflatable as it's so shallow. We had a soldier from Chickerell Camp once who got stuck up to his waist in the mud. It was a good exercise as the rescue involved the Coast Guard, police, us, the ambulance service and fire brigade, which luckily had an inflatable walkway. He'll have a good story to tell his friends. Occasionally drunks fall into the harbour and need hauling out. The other evening we were

Tuesday is RNLI crew night, for training and meetings. At the end of July, Lifeboat Week sees the crew put on a display with a helicopter and abseiling from Nothe Fort. The RNLI boat house is open during the day when manned and the shop is run by volunteers.

called out to help the police. They had arrested a drunk, who then escaped; as they now had a duty of care they were worried he might drown in the harbour. We found him shivering in a boat, suffering from hypothermia.'

Sea Rowing

Weymouth Rowing Club is a phoenix risen from the ashes of a tragedy. In 2000, Tristan Douglas-Johnson set out from his home excited at the prospect of a day out at Southampton International Boat Show. He never returned. At the age of 20 he was killed by a runaway RIB that had minutes before thrown all its occupants into the sea whilst on a demonstration run. Tristan was an affable young man, and it was his colleagues at Kingfisher Marine who came up with the idea of building not one but two Cornish pilot gigs as a long-lasting memorial to him. Friends and family rallied together and it was not long before they had a gig on the water and were racing.

There is a programme for new rowers to move through the ranks. Beginners row on Sunday mornings by appointment and juniors (aged 11–16) row Saturday mornings. Coach Sarah Fennell says, 'As long as they can reach the stretcher position and hold an oar they can row'.

The club is a registered charity and now has over 120 members, including around 30 youngsters. Sarah Fennell is a founder member, coach, cox and competitive rower:

'Weymouth was the first gig rowing club to be formed in Dorset. Gigs originate from Cornwall and the Isles of Scilly, lots of small towns there have them and people grow up with gig rowing in their community. When we first started competing, travelling miles to Cornwall, we didn't really know what we were up against and people joked about Weymouth bringing up the rear. But we're climbing the leagues now. In the 2011 World Championships, around 130 boats took part and our men's A crew came 16th and ladies' A crew 21st.

We train three times a week for 1–2 hours and there are regattas every other weekend during May to September, so it's quite a commitment. We organise an annual regatta at the Nothe, which is a big fundraiser. We also do interclub racing – mixed races for newer rowers as well as competitive rowers. But if you don't want to compete, that's okay too. There's a brilliant social side to rowing. There's nothing better than heading out into the bay after a hard day's work and rowing your cares away. It's addictive and very exhilarating.

The gigs are beautifully crafted boats, costing around £24,000 to build and kit out to racing specification. A Cornish pilot gig is 32 ft in length with a 4 ft 9 in beam. They are clinker built with elm or oak. Their specification is based on the Treffry, a gig built in 1838 and still in regular use by Newquay Rowing Club. Their original use was to take pilots out to incoming ships in the Atlantic approaches. The fastest gig would have the best chance of securing the pilotage fees. Originally a commercial venture, now the sport of gig racing has become established in the West Country and is spreading to Holland, France, the Faeroes, Australia and the USA.

The gigs take six rowers and a cox. We launch into a busy harbour so the coxswains are trained in the rules of the sea. Gusting easterly winds sometimes mean we can't launch, and white water in the harbour entrance can be a problem for the less experienced. But these boats were built to be raced out to the big ships so they are really robust.'

Trips from Weymouth

Ferries

It is possible to travel year-round from Weymouth to Guernsey (just over 2 hours), Jersey (just over 3 hours) and St Malo (from 5 hours) aboard Condor Ferries. The terminal on the Quay has information, maps and guides.

Small ferries leave for Portland Castle and Lulworth Cove. Terry Pavey has been taking people out in his boat around the breakwater for the last 22 years; his father did the same for 40 years, before handing over the reins. His boat *Lady Ella* (named after his granddaughter) can take 12 passengers, including animals. He was once asked to accommodate a tortoise that was going on a sea journey and its owner wanted to accustom it to water. Terry offers hourly trips with commentary between Easter and October. Around the breakwater you can still see old cannons that have tumbled off the wall onto the rocks below.

If looking for a shorter trip, to save the walk round to the Nothe, try the rowing ferry. A mere 50p buys you the strong arms of a ferryman in his traditional clinker boat. The job was originally kept for retired seafarers and fishermen, and today there are four men licensed by the Council to operate here. They pay to have their boats safety inspected, for a waterman's licence to prove they know the 'rules of the road' and also to use the public steps. Occasionally the tide is out and it's so shallow on the Weymouth side they can't get the boat alongside; it happens about twice a year with the spring tide. The ferry operates between Weymouth (Nothe Parade) and old Melcombe Regis (near the Pavilion), Easter to October weather permitting, 10 am till dusk.

Another small boat, *My Girl*, is a familiar sight in the harbour. Built in Cornwall in 1931, she had an important job during WWII carrying men,

(Photo courtesy of Paul Dallaway)

shells, guns and paraffin to the forts on the breakwaters. She was requisitioned by the Army at the outbreak of war. Today she is part of the Historic Ships Association of Great Britain and proudly flies her Royal Artillery pennant. You can still see shrapnel embedded in her timbers following a bombing raid. *My Girl* used to belong to Marian Lye's father Ron Hill. Ron died in 1991, shortly after the book *Weymouth at War: Ron Hill's Story of the Vessel My Girl* was published.

'I sat down with Dad just after he'd had his stroke and we wrote the book together. He was a quiet, unassuming man and a very skilled seaman. He came from a seafaring family and inherited My Girl from his father in Plymouth, where she worked as a pleasure boat taking passengers to see the warships at Devonport and for trips along the River Tamar. At the beginning of WWII, she was ordered to come to Weymouth to service the Breakwater Forts. She used to make three to four trips a day, sometimes more, ferrying soldiers, stores, ammunition, etc. Portland was a major naval base and came under heavy enemy fire, as did other installations around the harbours of Portland and Weymouth. With tons of ammunition and paraffin aboard (paraffin was used to keep the lights going), it was very risky sailing across the large open expanse of the harbour! Dad and his brother Bert ran her together until Bert was injured when a heavy crate fell on his leg. The wound became badly infected and, as antibiotics were unavailable then, his leg had to be amputated. After that, the Commanding Officer at the Water Transport Office sent various young lads to help crew. In 1944, My Girl played her part in the preparations for D-Day – Weymouth and Portland were key departure points for American troops involved in the liberation of Europe.

My parents' love story centred on the boat. My mother, Dolores, was a local girl, working as a postwoman in the area of Hope Quay and Bincleaves, and every day Ron would ask her if there were any letters for him from home, as Plymouth was being bombed out too. They were married in 1942. After the War, Dad helped decommission the forts, then set up staging near the Pier Bandstand on Weymouth Esplanade and My Girl went back to her previous role as a pleasure boat. She became known as 'The pleasure boat that went to war'. Paul Compton owns her now and he's a respected sailor, so she's in good hands.* Some soldiers from the Royal Artillery (who mainly manned the forts) come back each year for a trip. She and Dad inspired a lot of love and she was like one of the family; the boat came first as she put food on the table.

For the last years of his working life, Dad acted as co-pilot to two of the big vessels taking part in and winning the World Windspeed Championships – Crossbow and Crossbow II – owned by Tim Colman (of the Colman's Mustard family). Tim once said that Dad's knowledge of Portland Harbour – the winds and tides – won him their record-breaking successes. It was a fitting tribute.'

* Paul Compton used to command the *T.S. Pelican* and other tall ships based in Weymouth before he bought *My Girl*. The boat carries trippers along the coast and to Portland Castle from Easter until end of October; disembark at the Castle and return on any of her sailings. The ticket hut is the black-and-white-painted White Motor Boats kiosk on Cove Row. She takes group bookings, including wedding, hen and stag parties; some even make their last trip in her as relatives scatter their ashes in the bay.

The *Pelican*

When in Weymouth the *T.S. Pelican* moors alongside Custom House Quay near the Pavilion. 'The ultimate pirate ship', she started life in 1946 as a French fishing trawler in the Arctic and then was used as a Norwegian trader. In 1995, Graham Neilsen, a retired naval officer, bought the hull and converted her to a square-rigger. She is now a training ship, offering young people and adults the chance to learn and experience sailing with a permanent professional crew. Mike Forwood is one of a pool of captains. Mike travels from home near Tavistock, staying on board for days at a time. As captain, he is in charge of everyone on board and is responsible for ensuring the ship operates safely and within regulations. Having worked on tall ships like the *Pelican* for more than 25 years and prior to that as a deep-sea ferry captain trading around the world, he brings a wealth of experience. The ship also relies heavily on volunteers to help with repairs and maintenance. Andrew at one time was part of the team:

> 'During the four or so months she's back home (in Weymouth), I've been helping out. Anyone can volunteer – you don't need any special skills, though trade skills are a bonus. Bruce here is an engineer and electrician, others are carpenters. There's always cleaning, painting and sanding to be done. Some teenagers help out during the day, and lots of ex-crew come back; they fall in love with the boat and adopt the skipper as grandfather! Volunteers get free food and lodging on board, it's great experience and we have fun.'

Between April and December the *Pelican* offers a full programme – from day sails and Channel sails to Discover Scotland, 10-day adventures and

3-month return trans-Atlantic trips. 'Guests' enjoy ensuite cabins, heating, air-conditioning and three meals a day prepared by the ship's cook. According to one youngster, 'It was the best 24 days of my life'. She also takes part in the International Tall Ships Race, one of about five such UK vessels among the 150 ships that enter the race.

Charter Boats

The Weymouth angling charter fleet is said to be the largest in the country. The Deep Sea Directory (www.deepsea.co.uk) has information on local angling, diving and commercial charter boat operators and availability, special deals, competitions and boats for sale. A day's fishing on the banks or wrecks costs approx. £40–60 per person, and some skippers hire out rods and reels. David Pitman is an experienced fisherman and charter-boat skipper:

'I've been taking people out fishing for the last 40 years or so. I was born in Weymouth and when only 5 years old started going to sea with my father, a commercial fisherman. I left school at 15 to help him out. We used to do a few angling trips at weekends; then, 17 years ago, when I wasn't physically fit enough to continue commercial fishing, I started doing charters full-time. I've had many different boats over the years, including the first vessel to have Decca Navigator, which preceded GPS; this meant we could go further afield and find wrecks. I take people out who've never fished before, as well as regulars, and carry everything on board. We offer 8- and 12-hour trips and are licensed for 12 people, but normally run with 8 or 10.'

Most local sea anglers and charter-boat skippers have signed up to the 'Recycle Fish' scheme. This was formed by two conservation-minded skippers Dave Gibson (*Lady Godiva*) and Chris Caines (*Tiger Lily*) to encourage fishermen to take only the fish they intend to eat, using barbless hooks and 'catch and release'.

Swimming

Open-water swimming from Weymouth goes back a long way. The Weymouth Swimming Club was established in 1825, now based at the indoor pool at Knightsdale Road. The tradition of teaching open water swimming continues, with classes taking place during the school summer holidays in a designated area off the pier. Sea races are traditionally held during the summer every year. The British Heart Foundation charity swim occurs along the bay from the Pavilion end to the groyne near Lodmoor Country Park, a distance of 1 mile (1.6 km), with 500 or so swimmers usually taking part. The Lions Club Christmas Day Harbour Swim also attracts a surprising number of entrants and a huge crowd of onlookers. In 2010, 152 hardy souls were watched by up to 4000 spectators who lined the harbourside.

British Heart Foundation 2010 Weymouth Bay swim. (Photo courtesy of actionpic.co.uk.)

Local man Tom Watch (now in his 80s) has been coaching cross-Channel swimmers for over 60 years. One of his young swimmers was Mervyn Sharpe, who was crowned King of the Channel after swimming it no less than seven times, the last time in 1974. Tom's latest protégé is Somerset-girl Katrina Baker. Katrina says:

'I've always been a swimming pool competitor, then in 2008 I did a three-times chain relay Channel swim and I'm currently training for the solo crossing. Average time to swim the 22 miles (35 km) across the Channel is 12–14 hours. We'll set off from Shakespeare Beach or maybe Samphire Hoe (near Dover), depending on the tide, and ideally finish at Cap Griz Nez, Calais; the tide changes every 6 hours so you tend to drift and may not always end up exactly where you want to. You pay to register with the Channel Swimming Piloting Federation, who

then supply a boat and pilot. An observer ensures the swim is done legally – that you don't touch the boat and that you're not wearing a wetsuit or any padding. You can choose any stroke but should then stick with it all the way, as this is recorded.

The English Channel is the busiest shipping lane in the world. As a swimmer you simply follow the boat and the pilot makes sure the way ahead is clear. Besides the wash off the big ships, jellyfish can be a problem for some swimmers because they are allergic to their stings. And of course there's the cold – the water is only 14–18 degrees (compared to the usual 28/29 in a pool). I'll be 'greased up' to prevent chaffing and to give a little bit of insulation. You also have to be topped up every half hour or so with carbohydrates or else you start to lose energy. We use a plastic milk bottle which is passed out on a string while I tread water.'

Tom Watch explains how he got into coaching:

'I used to swim in the sea, as kids we all did – you learnt to swim by falling in the harbour. I wasn't a particularly great swimmer, but in 1951 a local guy, Geoff Chapman*, asked me to help him swim the Channel. "Channel Chapman" as we called him became the 23rd person to swim from France to England, and it just kind of followed on from there. I've coached swimmers from all over the world. We used to start training in February and they'd leave footprints in the frost on the Pier – the reason was to get them used to the cold. Setting off from France was the easiest option, but after some controversy between the pilots and the French, we were stopped, so nowadays we set off from England. We used to organise swims along the coast between Swanage and Weymouth. Lulworth to Weymouth was a 10.5-mile (16.9-km) course. And we'd take swimmers around Portland. But it's always possible to find a favourable place in Weymouth or Portland Harbour to swim. We also used to swim early season in Little Sea, as you could go in on the top of a tide and swim for about half an hour without moving from that spot, the tide was so strong. Japanese seaweed can be a bit of a nuisance around Newton's Cove. Taking Katrina out, we've been accompanied by basking sharks and porpoises – they like to follow the boat. I've been saying for years this'll be my last year coaching, but I seem to keep doing it. I still swim 100 lengths a week myself, though in the local swimming pool, not the sea!'

* Geoff Chapman still swims regularly in the sea, an enthusiastic member of Newton's Cove Wrinklies swimming club.

The Open Water Championships take place in Weymouth Bay during the first week of July, when more than a hundred swimmers set off from Greenhill. They follow a marked course ranging from 750 m to 10 km (6.2 miles), swimming around buoys parallel to the beach, approximately 100 m out depending on the tide.

Smuggling

'Free trading' (smuggling) was rife in the 'old' days. In 1576 even the Mayor of Melcombe Regis had shares in a smuggling vessel from Cherbourg, the Collector of Customs and searchers were said to be 'debauched', and packet boat crews ran spirits between the Channel Islands and Weymouth, together with silk and lace which was popularly sold to the growing number of rich visitors to the town. Corruption was endemic, though perhaps not as much as in nearby Poole. Even small rowing boats could cross the short distance from Weymouth to France, which is why the government at one time banned and burnt all boats with less than four oars.

Weymouth was a pivotal point for smuggling on the Dorset coast, and the first Customs House was built here on Custom House Quay. Possibly ten officers would have been stationed here, undertaking the hazardous job of policing the port. They were not averse to accepting bribes as gentle persuasion, rather than risk harm or even death trying to enforce the law. In the 1830s/40s, the 'trade' was still going on, though on a more limited scale and without the violence of earlier times. A period of free trade when

The elegant Custom House on the Quay is now the HM Coastguard Portland Maritime Rescue Co-ordination Centre.

tariffs on most goods were reduced or removed led to the practice being less attractive.

The Pike and Shot Company's *Smuggling Tour* is a great way to explore Weymouth's smuggling history (see 'Guided Tours and Re-enactments').

The following piece was written by Cass Jackson:
During the Olympic and Paralympic sailing competitions, everyone expects to see fair play. But back in the early 19th century, few local seafarers were sticking to the rules. Notorious gangs of smugglers ruled the waves. From the sailors who brought in the goods, through those who hid the contraband inland, and finally those who purchased the illicit cargo, most everybody was implicated. As Kipling's verse reminds us, there was '*Brandy for the Parson; 'Baccy for the clerk*'.

In reality, smuggling was not at all poetic. Smugglers were shot, if they could not be apprehended. His Majesty's Customs Officers fared no better. If they were outnumbered, the smugglers showed no mercy. In 1822, at least two officers were thrown to their deaths off the cliffs. On another occasion, the coastguards took to sea to prevent a vessel bringing contraband ashore. Their boat was deliberately run down by the smugglers and sank, with consequent loss of all hands.

Any Preventives (revenue men) captured by the smugglers were not always killed. Sometimes they were tied to their own horses. On being whipped the horses galloped away from the scene of the encounter and the Preventive was lucky if it stopped before he was miles inland. It is interesting to note that the Customs Management Act still states that 'The carrying away of an officer is an offence'. The most dangerous time for all was the point at which the illegal goods were being offloaded. A moonless night was best for this, but if the shore was moonlit, the customs men were most likely to strike. Many bloody battles took place and lives were lost on both sides.

If the goods were successfully landed, they were whisked away to be hidden until the heat was off or taken well inland to be distributed. If the cache was hidden locally, it could end up in the church – up in the belfry or down in a tomb. This was how the parson came by his brandy. For the price of a keg of cognac, farmers would help. The contraband was conveyed by mules, ponies and manpower to a meadow, where it was sunk into the ground. This was often in a pre-dug 'well', excavated in readiness. The soil and turf were then replaced and the spot marked in some way, even by planting a tree on top.

The revenue officers became aware of this practice and searched for newly replaced turf. Trying to keep one step ahead, the smugglers went round the fields creating false 'wells' in dozens of different places, hoping the revenue men would give up the search. This was a continuous and protracted 'game' between the two factions, each trying to outfox the other in what was literally a deadly strategy.

One of the most notorious smugglers at this time was Emmanuel Charles, landlord of a public house, the Crown Inn, at Osmington Mills, just outside Weymouth. It still stands (as the Smugglers Inn) away from the village and down a winding road, where a stream runs into the sea. One of Emmanuel's suppliers and a great friend was Peter Latour, a sailor known as French Peter. The story goes that John Tallman, a naïve young customs officer from Weymouth, visited the Crown Inn in the hope of persuading Emmanuel to help him capture the man. Emmanuel welcomed the young officer, plied him with brandy and set about telling him what a dangerous character Peter was – vile tempered and likely to cut anyone's throat if he felt like it. Definitely a man to be avoided.

It happened that French Peter was due to make a delivery that very day. When Emmanuel saw him approaching the inn, he pointed him out to Tallman – who appeared to have suddenly lost interest in this notorious individual. Indeed, he became so agitated that Emmanuel suggested he should hide in the chimney. No sooner had the young man disappeared than Latour came into the bar. Emmanuel offered him gin, instead of his usual brandy – apparently a secret code to indicate that something was amiss. The landlord put his finger to his lips and pointed to the chimney.

Quick to recognise the situation, French Peter said he'd prefer brandy to gin, and added that he would sit beside the fire, as he was feeling the sea-chill. The two men then proceeded to build up the fire with damp twigs, heather and rotting leaves producing a vast amount of smoke. It wasn't long before young Tallman tumbled into the hearth – soot-stained, coughing and choking. Hastily, he made his excuses and hurried back to Weymouth, with nothing to report.

Should you be taking a moonlit walk near the Smuggler's Inn and see a group of roughnecks approaching, be sure to turn away. Remember Kipling's verse – *'Them that asks no questions isn't told a lie, so watch the wall, my darling, while the Gentlemen go by'.*

The Seafront and Beach

Royal Visitors

It is commonly believed that the resort of Weymouth really got going in the 1800s after it became popular with Georgian socialites and the Royal Family in particular. Apparently the King was advised by doctors to stop 'taking the waters' at Bath, these being too acidic, and try Weymouth's, which he duly did, and the Royal Family went on to spend many summer holidays there. The King suffered from an unknown illness of the nervous system (porphyria) (hence his nickname Mad King George) and was advised to bathe in seawater to help his affliction.

However, according to local historian Martin Ball, the first time the King visited was on his Grand Tour of the South West, when he stopped off to visit the Duke of Gloucester. Apparently the King was forced to leave hurriedly after a failed assassination attempt, and subsequent visits were prompted by a need to quash unruly Republicans, not, sadly, to enjoy the pleasures of the seafront. Yet the King did spend at least four holidays in Weymouth. Moreover, it was owing to the need for some privacy for the King that 'bathing machines' became popular. The gently shelving beach and sand 'as smooth as a carpet and as firm as a rock' (Reeby 1995) were particularly easy for these horse-drawn huts, which were the only respectable means of entering the water in those days (as originally nude bathing was necessary for the cure to be effective). Men were forbidden to row near the machines for the sake of ladies' privacy. Larger saloon huts could accommodate up to 56 bathers in individual cabins. These huts were still being used until around 1900.

The King of course would have attracted a crowd. There is a reference in Thomas Hardy's *The Trumpet Major* to such an occasion:

> 'A group of florid men with fiddles, mandocellos, a trombone and a drum came forward, packed themselves into another bathing machine that was waiting and were drawn out into the waves to the King's rear … then a deafening noise burst from the bathing machine … It was the condensed mass of musicians inside striking up God Save the King as his majesty's head rose from the water.'

It was believed that the shock of a dip in cold water sent blood away from the body surface to inner areas to revitalise them and improve blood flow. Doctors advised 5 minutes full naked immersion every day for males and 2 minutes three times a week for delicate females and invalids, and that 'People whose extremities turned blue should leave the water at once'. There was no 'bathing season', hardy souls entering the sea at all times of the year.

The Seafront and Beach Today

Weymouth Bay has designated areas for different sea users – see noticeboards along the Esplanade:

- White buoys mark the safe swimming area and no-go zone for boats, etc. Beyond the white buoys the speed limit is 8 knots. Anchoring and unguarded propellers within 400 m of the shoreline are prohibited. Strong easterly winds tend to wash the buoys up on the beach, so during winter they are brought ashore.
- Red buoys mark the personal water craft (PWC) and jet-ski channel, only to be used for gaining access to the beach. Jet-ski craft should not enter Weymouth Harbour.
- Yellow buoys mark the sailboard approach channel.
- Blue buoys indicate where anchoring is permitted.
- Red and white buoys mark the ski-boat approach channel; this is only to be used to gain access to the beach.

In July and August no skating or skateboarding is allowed along the Esplanade, and at all times there is no cycling. In the summer lifeguards patrol the area, red and yellow flags denoting when they are on duty. Two swimming rafts are accessible in July and August.

Two miles (3.2 km) east of Weymouth is Bowleaze Cove. The beach and pier are fronted by a car park and family restaurant, the owners of which have the right to charge for use of the area (for deckchairs, boat launches, etc.). There is a small funfair, five-star holiday park and campsite, and the whole

area is dominated by the backdrop of the Riviera Hotel which is privately owned.

Preston Beach extends from Bowleaze Cove to Greenhill, officially ending just before the rock groyne near Lodmoor car park. The causeway was built in Victorian times; before that travellers had to venture all the way round the marshes to go west. The beach almost exactly faces the longest fetch of open water and is a storm beach (affected by particularly fierce waves). In 1995/6 new sea defences were built, the promenade was widened and shingle was imported to increase the size of the beach. Prior to this, road closures were common as storm-thrown shingle littered the highway.

View along Preston Beach towards Bowleaze Cove. (Photo courtesy of Richard Holmes.)

The largest pebbles are found here on Preston Beach, the sand becoming progressively finer towards the entrance to Weymouth Harbour. The town partly owes its growth and prosperity to its fine white sand. Like other bays that face east, Weymouth Beach never receives the full impact of big waves carrying shingle but instead attracts the deflected ends of the waves, loaded with sand.

Donkeys

Donkeys had been providing rides on Weymouth sands since Queen Victoria's time, thanks to one family – the Downtons – who eventually retired in 2000. There were a few years when the beach was donkey-less. Then in 2005 Maggie Aldridge started up a team of donkeys, until 2010 when Melanie Rush took over the reins of Maggie's eight donkeys. The donkeys work at the Pavilion end of the beach, providing children's rides throughout the season. Young jockeys can buy a rosette after their ride. Melanie uses Western saddles so the children feel safe as they have a horn to hold onto. The headpiece is a cross between a head-collar and bridle, and the donkeys are generally bit-less, apart from the odd day when they are feeling excitable. Melanie says:

'They don't usually drag you along the beach! The youngest are 7-year-olds Dainty and Daisy. Dainty only started as a beach donkey in mid-2010 and she had to get used to the noises on the beach. During D-Day celebrations when there were tanks around she jumped out of the enclosure in fright. But in most cases you could let a bomb off next to the donkeys and they'd hardly bat an eye. We took Dainty to a school fete and she was so excited, it was a case of information overload. She's a busy donkey, she likes to get on with it. Jasmine sets the pace, which is slow. Bee is really good with kids who may not sit still. Although the donkeys are all girls, sometimes they get a bit frisky and jump on each other's backs – that always causes some amusement; you have to watch for the signs. Sooty has been known to go off on a jolly. At a recent event she wandered off and thought it great fun having people chase after her.

I live in Sherborne and the donkeys are kept at Preston. Jane helps muck out, clear the field and keep an eye on them, she's really good support. My son Toby and daughter Bethany also help on the beach, with husband Tom behind the scenes (doing repairs, etc.). It's extremely hard work and you couldn't live off it, you really need a second income. It's hard to put into words how rewarding it is. A lot of children don't have contact with large animals and it's lovely to see their excitement; riding a donkey might be the highlight of their holiday. The worst thing is having to turn children away – we have a 7 st weight limit for the well-being of the donkeys – but then I sometimes let them help lead brothers or sisters.'

Sooty enjoying an Extra Strong Mint. 'She's really smart, she knows if the lunch-time sign goes out. She's also partial to going on strike!' says owner Melanie. The donkeys have won rosettes for Best Beach Donkeys, Best Individual Donkey and Best Trimmed Feet (an annual competition run by the Donkey Sanctuary, Sidmouth).

Punch and Judy

There has been a Punch and Judy show on Weymouth Beach since the 1880s. Punch and Judy originated in Italy in the 17th century and 2012 is Mr Punch's 350th birthday. Mark Poulton is the current Professor, taking over from Guy Higgins in 2005 who retired after 29 years, and Frank Edmonds before him who served an impressive 49 years. The shows have always been busked on the beach with the audience contributing money to the collector's hat or box, and it still works this way today. Mark says:

'I saw my first Punch and Judy show in the early 1970s at Weston-super-Mare, and the following year while on holiday in Weymouth I discovered Prof Guy Higgins "famous" Punch and Judy. I must have watched every performance for that week, excited by every show. At the end of that holiday I stated, "When I grow up I'm going to be a Punch and Judy man!" Then, in 1988, at the age of 16, I won the "Most Promising Puppeteer" award.

Today my shows are tailored to the audience but are essentially a cross between Carry On films and The Simpsons, with lots of double entendres and picking on people in the audience. I use a "swazzle" instrument to make my voice sound like Mr Punch (a tiny reed-like device which the showman conceals in his mouth and speaks through). My Mr P is similar to Basil Fawlty – he does things people would love to do or say to others but don't because they're too polite. I treat it like a busk – 20 minutes seems to suit most people's attention spans. I work the seafront for about 3–4 months during the summer, paying a licence fee for my pitch. There's been a pitch in the same spot since the 1940s. Out of season I do private bookings and puppet-making. I design and make all the puppets, props and theatres myself, including wood-carving, sign-writing and sewing the costumes and curtains. In 2009 Mr Punch and I were presented to the Queen on Weymouth Beach.

I had one incident a few years back when a man decided that he would tell my collectors that P&J should be banned. He made a big song and dance about it. To cut a long story down, I told my collector that if he came back, to invite him to talk over his concerns with me. So, when he did we had a chat and he got his views aired. I asked him if he had ever watched one of my shows, which he hadn't, so told him to sit and watch one (which he did). The next day he turned up at the show with a bottle of wine and apologised – he said he had no idea that P&J could be like that! People do have preconceptions about the show, which is not the same as it was 100 or 200 years ago.'

Don't miss Mark's unique performances on the beach during Easter and from the end of May onwards throughout summer.

Sand Sculpting

Another unique thing about Weymouth's sea front is the sand sculpting. Resident sculptor Mark Anderson's creations are works of art – see the chapter 'The Arts' and 'Family Fun and Other Activities' for how he does it.

The Land Train

The land train has been a familiar sight along the Esplanade for years. The current train is a Treni Dotto Italian-made convoy, registered in 1994 and built of fibreglass with a steel chassis. The 4-cylinder Perkins diesel engine is coupled to a Ford Transit gearbox and it has air-assisted brakes and a wheelchair ramp. The train carries up to 40 people (and dogs) comfortably and leaves on the hour from Lodmoor and on the half hour from the King's Statue. Sue and Trish dispense tickets from an ancient bus ticket machine, while Richard and Keith are the main drivers.

Richard says, 'It drives like a big garden tractor. The trip takes 10–15 minutes at 5–6 mph safe speed, although it can go faster, and it is road legal. We have a whistle, bell and beacon lights to let people know we're coming.'

Nature Areas

Weymouth has some large, unique natural areas very close to the town centre.

Radipole Lake

Radipole Lake is a wetland paradise and birdwatchers' mecca of reedbeds, ditches, fens, marshes and shallow lagoons. Over a dozen species of mammal live here, including water voles and otters – absent after almost 30 years and encouraged to repopulate the area by the use of artificial holts. Piles of wood chippings and soil provide refuge for amphibians, and there is a sand martin 'hotel' and numerous bat roosts. Nearly 40% of Britain's bat species have been seen flitting around the reserve, including the nationally rare Nathusius' pipistrelle.

Rubble from war-bombed areas of town was used to construct the paths, and the odd fruit tree around the reserve is a throw-back to this. Original water ditches were 6 ft wide by 6 ft deep, but over the years these have gradually filled in and required restoration. Some have been profiled to make them shallower and easier for wildlife to get to the water's edge, some redug with straight sides, while others have been allowed to dry out a little to encourage a variety of plant species to flourish, and some of the dominant reeds have been ousted in favour of sedges – all measures designed to enhance biodiversity. The reed beds are cut on a rotational basis, mostly on a 5-year cycle, but there are plans to reintroduce shorter rotation cutting to use the

The RSPB is continually maintaining and improving access to the nature reserve, for instance with new pond-dipping and duck feeding platforms.

reed for thatching houses, the first time this will have happened for nearly 40 years! New dragonfly ponds have been created, and it is hoped that the 4 miles (7 km) of restored ditches and 0.8 acre (2 ha) of newly created open water will encourage more wildlife. Also unobstructed lines of sight enable visitors to see the wildlife more easily.

Human visitors are not the only holiday-makers who come here; over 260 bird species have been recorded here, some wholly dependent on reedbeds for their survival, for instance sedge and grasshopper warblers and bearded tits. Marsh harriers (rarer than golden eagles) have nested here and reared young, the first to do so in Dorset for nearly half a century. A pair was first seen in 2009 'sky dancing' and shortly afterwards three young were seen on the wing in July. Fingers are crossed that these wonderful birds will continue to return to breed in future springs. The bittern is another of our rarest birds, perfectly camouflaged for living amongst reeds. The RSPB is encouraging volunteers to listen out for the male's distinctive booming call which sounds like a foghorn and can carry up to 3 km. 'Boomers' are most often heard just before dawn in spring and early summer.

Daniel Bartlett is the Senior Visitor Centre Assistant:

'The RSPB is here to maintain the habitat, and we also want to introduce people to our work. We maintain a healthy fish population to keep other wildlife happy. Carp are bottom-feeders and stir up silt which has a detrimental effect on water quality, so we have installed fish fences to exclude them from certain areas, constraining them to the areas where the local anglers can get at them! We have worked with the local angling club to help them install platforms at the bottom end of Swannery Car Park and along Radipole Park Drive where fishing is allowed, in season, with a permit.

We've installed a pond-dipping platform and nest-box cameras. The duck feeding platform is designed to allow feeding over the water, which is better for

From the windows of the Centre, you can use the binoculars and telescope to view the wildlife on the Lake.

the waterfowl and discourages vermin. We encourage people to buy a small bag of bird seed, to gently steer them away from feeding white bread which isn't good for the ducks. A hooded merganser has been living here for several years (of unknown origin), and our 'hoodie' has become a bit of a celebrity, though he sometimes goes on holiday to Poole Park.'

As well as regular guided walks around the reserve, there are special events such as bug hunts and bird searches. Explorer backpacks can be borrowed from the Centre, as well as bird bingo sheets and treasure trails, great ways for younger visitors and their parents to enjoy the reserve's wildlife. Digital video cameras link back to the Centre, with otters and foxes captured on film.

There is no cycling allowed on the tracks as they are public footpaths, although dogs are welcome on a lead. The Lake area is open all year round and the hide from 8.30 am to 4.30 pm. Keep up to date with reserves sightings and news by visiting www.rspb.org.uk/weymouthwetlandsblog or www.twitter.com/rspbweymouth.

A small area in the lower reaches of the lake is one of the home waters of the local **Model Boat Club** (as well as the Sea Life Centre and Mangerton Mill near Bridport). Sail, electric-powered and steam-powered craft might be spotted here. They meet at St Nicholas Church Hall, Buxton Road, on the first Tuesday of the month at 7.30 pm. Contact 01305 834668 for more information.

Lodmoor

In earlier times, 'Everyone with a gun and a taste for letting it off knew Lodmoor', according to John Meade Falkner (author of *Moonfleet*). In the

The circular route of 2 miles (3.2 km) through Lodmoor reserve is pushchair-friendly and dogs are welcome on leads.

1960s, this nature area was seriously being considered as a Butlins holiday camp site, as it was regarded by locals as an unappealing wilderness, useful only for the dumping of rubbish. Today this grazing marsh has ditches, shallow pools, reed beds and native shrubs and is a haven for wildlife and local people. Bearded tits and Cetti's warblers live here all year round, together with a large colony of common terns in summer. Many species of waders can be seen during autumn, and in winter lapwing, golden plover, snipe, pintail, teal, wigeon and shoveler ducks. You may also see deer.

Lorton Meadows

Tucked away down the end of Lorton Lane, just past Littlemoor Road, is the Dorset Wildlife Trust Nature Reserve of Lorton Meadows. It is surrounded by housing and the new relief road and so offers an oasis for people and nature. The 14-acre (34-ha) site is an area of unimproved grassland with great views. The Wildlife Centre is open from April to October and has wildlife displays, a small shop, toilets, a picnic area and parking (with disabled facilities). Webcams are trained on bird nests, and sometimes barn and tawny owls, great tits and kestrels are captured on the television screens. The grassland attracts a variety of butterfly species, including marbled white, common and holly blues, and small and large skippers. You may be lucky to see bee orchids, which only flower once every 5–8 years, in June/July. During school holidays and some weekends, the centre offers family activities and guided walks.

The Nothe

The gardens on the Nothe have outstanding views of Portland Harbour and plenty of places to sit in quiet contemplation. The robins and grey squirrels are so tame they may eat out of your hand, while mammals hide in the long grassland and wooded areas, which are left as natural as possible to encourage wildlife. There are plenty of species to interest bird-watchers, including blackcap and chiffchaff which overwinter here. Near the water's edge, look for oyster catchers, turnstones, black redstart and common sandpiper, which overwinter in its shelter; also British divers (the bird kind) and eider duck. The area is nationally important for red-breasted mergansers. Train your binoculars on the breakwaters

to spot gulls and terns which nest there. Water birds such as cormorant and shag are found at any time of the year, as well as great-crested, black-necked and Slovenian grebe. In some winters, the less common little auk or black guillemot may be seen. Pipistrelle and noctule bats (Britain's largest bat) come out at dusk.

The Nothe provides a mixture of habitats and the aim is to preserve this diversity. The sandstone at Newton's Cove has weathered into vertical joints, giving it a 'pavement effect', which is great for rock-pooling.

A local guy called Mac regularly comes to feed the birds. He tells the story of how he started with 'Jimmy', an orphaned young sparrow and how the other sparrows would sit watching until they plucked up courage to come down to him. Jimmy turned out to be female, as she brought two young with her the next year, then no more. Starlings have been coming ever since and are so tame they land on Mac. His entourage also includes pigeons and a couple of crows. He swims in the Cove and has done so regularly for nigh-on 30 years: 'The water numbs the pain in my hip for a while. I've only been to the pool once – but never again! It's too hot and crowded.' His electric bike helps him get about now.

Chesil Beach and the Fleet

The Fleet is the largest saline lagoon in the UK, at 8 miles (12.9 km) long. The fact that one end joins the Isle of Portland to the mainline makes it a tombolo. The shingle bank is 12 m above high water at Portland, sloping to 6 m at the Bridport end. Old smugglers pulling up on the beach on a dark night could tell roughly where they were from the size of the pebbles, as they grade from west (pea-shingle) to east (cobble-sized). Pebbles are mostly flint and limestone, with some black chert and quartz.

As the tide falls and exposes the foreshore, fossils turn up, especially ammonites, belemnites, brachiopods and sea urchins. It is also a good time to spot anemones, sea squirts, crabs and other underwater living creatures. Eel grass supports large numbers of worms and shellfish, as well as providing a nursery and feeding ground for flatfish and gobies. The Fleet is one of Western Europe's most important marine nature reserves because of its sheltered waters and good food supply, and it has been managed as a bird-life centre since 1393. Watch out for Brent geese, widgeon, red-breasted merganser, goldeneye and red-throated divers, among others. From 1 April to 31 August the central section of Chesil Beach facing into the Fleet is closed for the little tern and ringed plover to breed. Vegetation such as yellow-horned poppy, sea kale and sea pea add splashes of colour in season. Mute swans flock here to graze on their favourite seaweed.

The *Fleet Observer*, with its glass bottom and special shallow draught designed for the lower reaches, offers hour-long trips with a local skipper who will tell you all about the history, geology, natural history and industrial uses of the area.

Contact the Chesil Beach Centre on Portland Beach Road for details of events, activities and talks throughout the year.

Bennett's Water Gardens and Chickerell Downs

Bennett's Water Gardens on Putton Lane off Chickerell Link Road are one of Europe's oldest water lily nurseries, with more than 150 species of lily. The gardens cover 6 acres (2.4 ha) and offer a tranquil place to indulge the senses. Water drains downhill naturally from Montevideo House and nearby Crook Hill, feeding the ponds, and the water level is fairly constant (a 'bung' in the big lake allows the level to be controlled if necessary). The gardens have always been family run. Angie Bennett explains how it all came about:

'In 1958, my father-in-law took over the old brickworks site. He was a hobby water gardener and was attracted to the ponds there. The clay is ideal for lilies, they thrive in it; in fact they sold so well he couldn't keep up with demand, so in 1978 he and my husband Jonathan got the diggers in and dug more lakes. At one time we had 30 pickers/harvesters and the water was solid with lilies. Then in the '80s prices fell as there was more competition, so we diversified by landscaping the gardens, providing a tea room and charging people to go round the gardens (it had been free before). We're now a major tourist attraction and are licensed for weddings. We still sell lilies in the shop and by mail order, but no longer do wholesale. The emphasis has changed and now we want reflection in the ponds so we keep areas free of lilies. Aquatic places are less fashionable these days and dying out. All the planting is natural, it's not too contrived; we keep the grass paths nicely cut and level, but you walk by wild flowers and nettles and there are weeds in the pond. We like to encourage wildlife and you might see the odd

rabbit or deer about.

Our link with Monet comes from the fact that the first water lilies my father-in-law planted came from Marliac nursery in Bordeaux, where Monet bought his plants for his garden in Giverny. In 1999 there was a big Monet exhibition in London and Monet-mania was the thing, so we commissioned a local carpenter, Sean Bartlett, to design and construct our own Monet bridge. Painting groups like to sit and paint the scene – the lilies are the same type Monet would have painted.'

The willow walk is a favourite with wedding photographers.

The ponds also attract mallards, tufted ducks, great crested newts and vivid blue dragonflies.

The Gardens are open April to September 10 am to 5 pm. April is a time of beautiful reflections, golden weeping willows, yellow marsh marigolds, cowslips and daffodils, and the first moorhen and coot babies. In winter little egrets roost in the trees. Watch for the flash of a kingfisher and the herons, which are so used to people they don't bother to fly off.

Just east of the Gardens is Chaffey's Lake – a wild area of reeds and bog which feeds into Radipole Lake. There is also a Woodland Trust site in this area. Turn left out of the Gardens and a short way up

Putton Lane there is an entrance to Chickerell Downs, a 12.6-acre (5.1-ha) wild area of broad-leaved trees, wetlands and ponds sandwiched between houses; as such it is an important public open space and wildlife area. It was once part of the Putton Lane Brickworks site which closed in 1965. The vast deposits of clay led to two brickworks being sited in this area. The other, Crook Hill Brickworks, closed in 1969. At the peak of production Crook Hill produced 100,000 bricks per week.

Wild About Weymouth and Portland

The RSPB, Dorset Wildlife Trust, local council and Natural England are collaborating over a project that aims to enable more people to value and make use of the borough's unique natural environment. You can get involved as a volunteer, undertaking practical work, part of which is making places physically easier to access. A legacy trail is part of the project – from Lorton Nature Reserve through Lodmoor, along the sea front to Radipole, along Rodwell Trail to Ferrybridge, on to the top of Portland, and through the quarries to the Bill. Along the way, stations provide information on all the walks from that point, so you can explore different areas, using existing footpaths and linking them together. Artists, sculptors and performing artists roped into the project will make it a great community resource.

Local Fare

As expected, Weymouth does great fish and shellfish. The popularity of the annual Seafood Festival is testament to this, with food demonstrations from top chefs. Mackerel, squid (quidling), plaice from the banks, crab, hand-dived scallops, lobster

and samphire are regularly on the menu of local eateries. Bennett's on the Waterfront fish and chip shop has risen to the challenge of local celebrity chef Hugh Fearnley-Whittingstall and added mackerel to their menu. Get to know a local fisherman for fish and shellfish straight off the boat.

Markets

- Farmers' market: Westham Bridge, second Sunday of the month, 10 a.m. to 3 p.m.
- General market: Swannery Car Park, weekly on a Thursday from Easter to October.

Some Local Producers/Retailers

Fantastic Sausage Factory, St Mary's Street

Dennis Spurr claims he ran the largest butcher's shop in the country in London before moving to Weymouth and opening his Fantastic Sausage Factory. His cheeky, controversial style often gets him into trouble. With the run-up to the Olympics, he put up his own special sign in the form of coloured rings of sausages, but was told to take it down because it was a misuse of the Olympic logo. This attracted national media attention with headlines such as 'Small-town butcher bullied by Olympic Committee'.

'Yes, I'm a bit of a cheeky chappie, but people seem to like that. I'm often stood outside the shop, handing out samples and giving some banter. We sell around 3 tons of sausages a week and everything is made here to my recipes – 30 different flavours, all with names [examples include the Tom Jones (pork and leek), Vampire Slayer (mushroom and garlic) and Godfather (Sicilian herbs and sun-ripened tomatoes)] – I like to see people smile when they read the signs. We also play upbeat music to make our customers happy. I like doing things for the kids too. We take part in the Weymouth Witch Hunt at Halloween, getting dressed up. The kids must find all the wicked witches who've turned the grown-ups into monsters, save us and turn us back. I earn a nice living from Weymouth and it's good to give something back.'

Helen's Famous Wholefoods, St Mary's Street

Helen was born in Osmington Mills and started as a market-stall holder, travelling the south coast, before opening a shop in Weymouth in 1986. She still has a weekly stall at Dorchester Market. Her husband grows plants for the stall and shop and her daughter helps out on Saturdays. Helen's is a treasure-trove of foods from around the world and also stocks many local products – eggs from Coldharbour, cheese from Denhay Farm, teas from Blendings (Poole) and Clippers (Bridport), bread from Shelley's (Dorchester), bread and cakes from Ceres (Yeovil) and watercress from Bere Regis. The shop building is listed and prior to the 1960s sold teas; an old Home & Colonial sign hangs just inside the front door. The passageway down one side used to go through to St Thomas Street, but like many others is now blocked. Pat helped Helen in the shop from the outset and is still there, making cakes and Christmas puddings after 25 years. Her daughter was one of her first Saturday girls.

Phoenix Bakery, 6–7 Coburg Place

Phoenix Bakery is jointly owned by Aidan Chapman and Lisa Chapman, who together have developed a novel concept for Weymouth – a high-street artisan bakery. Master Baker Aidan makes 'real bread' from his premises and is often on show in action in the large front window.

'I like people to be able to see what I'm doing. I start baking at 7 am on weekdays and as early as 1 am on Saturday, our busiest day, when we make more diverse breads and do a wholesale round, including supplying places like River Cottage. We use local, organic ingredients where we can, plus seasonal produce. Everything is made on the premises by hand. Our best-sellers are the brownies, eccles cakes, health bars and bruschettas.'

Upstairs on the walls of the simple café are local artists' work, which changes monthly. People meet here for weekly language classes. Aidan also runs baking classes for beginners and apprentices. He teaches his staff to bake so they know the products intimately and can be as passionate about them as he is.

Oyster Farm, Fleet Lagoon

There have been oysters farmed in the Fleet since Victorian times, when oysters were so commonplace and cheap that poor people could afford them and they were even used as animal fodder. Nigel Bloxham runs the current farm with his father-in-law David Scott.

Nigel is also executive chef/proprietor of the on-site Crab House Café. In 2005 Nigel took over and cleared the remains of the previous farm, installing eco-friendly timber posts and rails on which are hung baskets of developing oysters. Washed by the ebb and flow of the tide, the oysters are rolled around inside the baskets, just as they would be on the sea bed. This results in a smoother shell and fatter meat. After 7–15 months, the developed oysters are harvested. The farm provides a year-round supply and Portland oysters have a characteristic sweet, slightly briny taste owing to the chalky waters that run off the surrounding hills. They are predominantly sold in the Crab House Café and to other local restaurants. Charlie, Nigel's son and General Manager of The Crab House, explains:

'We're not a big operation – it's labour-intensive, but that way we ensure a premium product (we don't do wholesale to large companies or supermarkets). We farm Pacific oysters as we have found the native oyster does not react well to farming (they're more prone to disease). We buy most of our oysters between very small seed and approx. 1 year old. As they grow, they are thinned out into bigger-sized baskets. CEFAS (the local DEFRA marine science centre) checks the water every week and takes oysters away for testing, but the Fleet has B-Class water which is very clean. Before consumption, oysters are put in the purification tanks for 48 hours and UV light is passed through the water to kill any E. coli.

The Crab House Café menu changes twice a day due to the fresh fish being landed by local fishermen. All our fish is landed from Poole to Brixham and we work closely with a couple of small fishermen working out of the Fleet Lagoon,

Charlie (General Manager) says, 'There's a holding area close to the shore, but the main farm is in deeper water. When the tide is out we can walk over to the oysters; at other times we use waders and a flat barge to go down the rows. Weed has to be cleaned off to maintain a flow of food to the oysters.' The coast path here skirts the farm and hugs the Fleet to Langton Herring.

scallop divers, plus local crab and whelk boats in Weymouth. Tamarisk Farm at West Bexington supplies our salad and Just Good Stuff selects from local farms and brings us their own produce. In the Café dishes are cooked in front of the customer and you can choose your own live lobster. Our Crustastun in the tank room uses a single electric shock to stun the crustacean, then a longer one to kill the animal; this is the most humane way of killing crabs and lobsters and that way all the liquid stays in the crab and the meat is much sweeter. Crabs cracked at the table with hammer, board and bib are popular – it's very hands on!'

Weyfish, Custom House Quay

Since 1987, Weyfish has been selling fish from Custom House Quay, aptly from the old Fish Market; prior to that the building was used as a council hardware store. Colin, who used to be a local fisherman, runs the business with two processors and three counter staff:

'We do retail and wholesale, supplying hotels and restaurants locally, as well as places in Bridport, Lyme Regis and Swanage; we even export to Spain. We buy catches direct off Weymouth vessels and can keep up to 5 tonnes of live shellfish in our tanks until they're ready to be sent somewhere. We only take out what we

Fishmonger Tim sorts lobster, spider and brown crabs in the tanks out back. Steve works mostly in the shop front: 'We try to keep a good selection of fish on the counter, and summer visitors especially like the shellfish bar.'

need to cook up for the day. Fishermen are paid on weight each week and we have about 10 regular suppliers. I go to Billingsgate once a week, mostly taking crab and lobster and some wet fish, bringing back haddock, mussels, kippers and oysters. If we have too many of one type of fish, I may take them to Plymouth market.'

Weymouth Deli, 3 Frederick Place

Rugby player Lian Berry moved from Manchester to start his own deli business in Weymouth, which he runs more or less single-handedly.

'I stick to fairly traditional methods, making 95% of the fresh stuff myself – all the pies, pasties, sausages and faggots, even down to the pastry. We also bone and cook all our own hams and meats on the premises. We sell local products – bacon and Cheddar cheese from Denhay Farms, Bridport; Blue Vinny from Woodbridge Farm, Sturminster Newton; Dorset Red Smoked Cheddar from Forde Farm at Abbotsbury. The Dorset Pate was made in Dorchester for over 70 years until the guy sold the recipe; it's now made in Hurn near Christchurch. We also sell clotted cream, ice cream and milk from Craig's Farm at Osmington, honey from Hogben at Broadmayne, Moores and Fudges biscuits, Dorset Preserving Company Ginger (cordial) and loose teas and coffee beans in tins that are probably older than I am!'

Sgt Bun Bakery, Lanehouse Rocks Road

Winners of the Western Region Bakery Championships, Val and Ian Temple have been running Sgt Bun, a traditional family bakery, since 1981. Their dedication to the business is impressive. Ian works nights (10 pm till 5 am), getting the bread and rolls ready for the day. His Jones oil-fired ovens have been in use for over 70 years. The day staff come in at 5 am to finish the icing, jamming and creaming and make the confectionery lines. Ian says, 'Most of our customers are local pensioners who appreciate home-produced bread, and passing tradesmen, but the trade is slowing so we've had to diversify more into cakes'. Their Belgian buns and range of muffins and flapjacks are popular, and their unique and delicious 'Bee Stings' are made from an old Austrian baker's secret recipe. 'Some years ago someone complained to Trading Standards that our pink-iced "Pig tarts" didn't contain any pork! After a piece in the *Echo*, we got national coverage.' They offer bread-making courses and are also known for their novelty birthday cakes, which can be made to order.

As well as being a Master Baker, Ian is Wildfox, a Druid belonging to the **Dorset Grove** (www.dorsetgrove.co.uk). He founded the Order in 2006, based on an earlier smaller faction, and it is open to anyone over the age of 18 and to both sexes. People come from as far as Portsmouth. All are environmentalists as druidry has a strong earth-based connection. Once a month they hold ritual meetings and also visit spiritual places to celebrate different Sabbaths. Popular places are Knowlton Church, Maiden Castle, Kingston Russell Stone Circle and along the South Dorset Ridgeway, for instance on the hill above Portesham where there is a quarry with an unusual dragon sculpture and inspiring views. Many of these places are chosen because of their energy, usually to do with ley lines. Greenhill and Bowleaze are other energy points where people still sense a connectedness with the Earth.

The Arts

Some Famous Artists

Famous artists have been attracted to Weymouth over the centuries. In 1811 **Turner** painted Weymouth Bay and sketched from the crest of the Ridgeway. **John Constable** also produced two famous paintings of the bay, one viewed from the Riviera Hotel looking along the beach to Overcombe Corner, showing the little River Jordan spilling out at Bowleaze. In 1816, while honeymooning at Osmington vicarage, he found time to sit atop the hills around Sutton Poyntz, painting the view. Landscape painter **John Upham** (1772–1828) was similarly drawn to this high vantage point on the old Roman road.

Described as 'the greatest history painter this Kingdom has ever produced', the artist **Sir James Thornhill** was born at the present White Hart in lower St Alban Street. He was appointed the King's Serjeant-Painter, tasked with overseeing the decorative work at the royal residences, from staterooms to stables. In 1722 he became Weymouth's MP, and was the painter Hogarth's father-in-law. His painting of *The Last Supper* graces St Mary's Church in St Mary Street.

Thomas Girtin (1775–1802) visited Weymouth and sketched the ancient houses in Maiden St (Ricketts 1976, p.98). Girtin was a renowned Romantic landscape painter and a friend and rival of Turner. He died of consumption at the age of 27 and his early death reportedly caused Turner to remark, 'Had Tom Girtin lived I should have starved'.

Samuel Prout painted landscapes and architecture and taught Turner, Gainsborough, Constable and Ruskin. Among his *Picturesque Views of the Southern Coast of England* is a painting of *Weymouth Castle, Dorsetshire* (Sandsfoot).

William Daniell was a landscape and marine painter. He also travelled the coast to paint inspirational views. His book *A Voyage Round Great Britain* (1814–25) has a painting of ships and boats in Weymouth Bay.

Visual Art in Weymouth

Artwey

Artwey was formed in 2008 as a focal point for Weymouth and Portland visual artists. Each year, members open their doors to showcase their work in the form of exhibitions, open studios and community events; it's a chance to meet and talk with artists, see their creations and share their inspirations. A route map is available from the TIC and other outlets. Andrea Frankham Hughes was a founder of the group:

'We (Clare Buckle, Olivia Nurrish, Sarah Gilpin, Bill Crumbleholme – one of the Upwey Potters – and myself) had all just done Dorset Art Week and felt that Weymouth and Portland were rather overlooked culturally, yet a lot of us were working as resident artists. Also many artists come here, inspired by the light and scenery. We wanted to raise the profile of Weymouth and Portland, to link artists together so they could network and share information. As the local area organiser for Dorset Art Week, I was well-placed to help set up a local group. We receive some community help, support from local businesses and some funding, but apart from that Artwey is voluntarily run – it's very hands on.

The website is a resource for all the artists involved, past and present. We are very open – there is no selection process – allowing upcoming artists to be mentored by more experienced ones. It's an exciting opportunity for new/ emerging artists to share ideas. We also want to demystify art, to let the local community see artists at work, talk to us and buy local art at reasonable prices. Some of us exhibit individually, some collectively; quite a number run courses and workshops, so people can have a go and learn skills from us.'

Some Local Artists

One of many venues that hosts Artwey artists is the Full Gamut Art Gallery & Coffee House in Chickerell Road, the creation of owner and curator Kimberley MacKeown, a Canadian artist who came to Weymouth 10 years ago.

'I feel it's vital to show visual art as something tangible for people to interact with and respond to, not just to promote it online, so I provide a space where fellow artists and I can showcase our work. I select work that is innovative and demonstrates the artist's aptitude with their chosen medium, quite apart from their experience level or training. I must also be convinced that the work will have broad appeal and be competitively but fairly priced. It's challenging to sell handmade/luxury goods in the midst of a recession, but many customers are thankfully tired of the false economy presented by cheaply manufactured imports, and I feel it's more important than ever to spotlight creative ingenuity and resourcefulness. Artists by nature are producers, not necessarily great promoters, so I assist by providing both a publicly accessible, supervised space and working full-time as a marketing agent to promote the artists who I represent. As I know the artists personally I can talk with gallery visitors about their work and production methods. This introduction to how art is made can help visitors better understand (and appreciate) the time, effort and resources that get invested by artists in their creations.'

On the wall inside the Gallery is one of local artist Ian Dyke's vibrant semi-abstract paintings (acrylic on canvas): 'After the Full Gamut show I entered three of my paintings in the Dorchester Open Art competition and got first prize, so I guess Kim knows what she's looking for when it comes to selecting for her tucked away little gallery!'

Despite being a small space, the Gallery offers a range of different ways for people to access visual art, learn more about it and get involved in creating themselves. There is free entry to the ongoing exhibitions, which rotate regularly, special activity days and a regular crafters' club evening. Kimberley offers bespoke workshops for small groups on request in a range of different media. 'It's lovely to see families, friends and often complete strangers interacting and doing a craft activity together. I've also been teaching a group of teens in an after-school art class. This has proved a great success, with the kids bouncing ideas off one another and expanding their artistic horizons. This young group of students is really inspirational and reminds me every week what it's all about – unbridled imagination!'

In summer you may see **Mike Taylor**, a resident watercolour artist on the Esplanade; since 1990 he has had a stall near the King's Statue. A Brummie, Mike fell in love with Weymouth and his artwork is inspired by the Jurassic Coast.

'I paint from photos, old postcards and on location, though don't sketch

or paint when manning the stall – I find I'm busy enough with customers and don't need to pull them in! My little humorous books are popular, including Dave the Famous Weymouth Seagull. I also do commissions and caricatures of celebrities. A lot of customers come back each year to see my new work, and people often comment that looking at one of my pictures on their wall reminds them what a great holiday they had in Weymouth. So I feel I'm a good ambassador for the town, encouraging people back. My fridge magnets are useful that way too. I romanticise Weymouth, but I think that's how visitors see it.'

Steve Bithell is a member of Dorset Visual Arts. Inspired by Constable and Camille Pissarro, Steve paints landscapes and seascapes in oils. He is interested in the changing landscape (whether changed by nature or man or

both) and, before the relief road was built, captured some of the views that would be lost and has also painted scenes along the coast from Portland to Lyme Regis. He is especially concerned about rapeseed in the English countryside:

'Rapeseed is very invasive. About 10/15 years ago it was very unusual to see a field of rape, now it's everywhere. The challenge for me as a landscape painter following the English tradition is to convincingly use so much of this acidic, unnatural looking colour. It's quite a challenge to paint it, the yellows seem wrong.'

Alistair Hampson is a local graphic designer and artist who is fascinated by the Georgian and Victorian architecture of the town. He works with pen and ink and also draws in Adobe Illustrator to capture the intricacies of the detailing on the buildings. He experiments with landscape photography using Photoshop artistic filters, and is also a signmaker.

Sand Sculpting

Weymouth has a long tradition of sand sculpting going back to Victorian times. 'Swift Vincent' was one of the first sand men on Weymouth Beach, retiring *c* 1930. Jack Hayward (1930s to early 1960s) specialised in cathedrals and architectural reproductions and for 70 years (1925–95) Fred Darrington made his livelihood creating sand sculptures; his forte was animals, especially monkeys playing cards and being mischievous, but most people will remember his amazing, life-like food, a peeled banana, apples, a loaf of bread, etc., the seahorses and his most commented on piece of sand art, a reproduction of Leonardo's 'Last Supper'. Current sculptor Mark Anderson (Fred's grandson) reckons Weymouth has the best sand in the world for modelling ('compared to most other sands it's like butter'). In the 1970s, Mark spent his days on the beach with his mother running the trampolines and his grandfather drawing the crowds with his unique sand sculptures. From the age of 11, Mark's summer job was to assist his grandfather, chiefly as water boy, postcard seller and money collector. Fred was 86 when he handed over the reins to Mark in 1988.

'To start with my work was pretty rubbish, but I was quite determined and gradually over a couple of years got better and get a little better each year. I became my grandfather's apprentice at age 22 and knew I'd succeeded when I turned up for work one day to find the sign had changed to "Sand Sculptures by FG Darrington & Grandson Mark". My grandfather usually started the season with sea horses, which took him a week to complete and usually lasted a further three; he didn't pack it down like I do and the wind would gradually excavate it. I take 6 weeks to make a sculpture, while he'd do one a month. His were more representational (he'd create out of his head) whereas I take a popular image and accurately reproduce it. I like to fine-tune.

I do paid commissions and some top world events. When the Queen visited in 2010 I was commissioned to create Windsor Castle. Sand sculpting is my choice for a pleasant way of life, it's like getting back to basics. It's second nature to me as I've been involved since I was very young. Beach sand sculpting is part of the heritage of Weymouth. My grandfather spent his life doing it and I value it tremendously.'

See Mark at work on Weymouth Beach during the summer opposite Alexandra Gardens and at Sand World, Lodmoor (www.sandworld.co.uk). His website (www.sculptureinsand.com) has useful tips on how to make the perfect sand castle. See more about Sand World in the section 'Family Fun and Other Activities'.

Books and Authors

The Elizabethan novel ***The Poisoned Cup*** is a Romeo and Juliet-style story of bitter local family strife, not surprisingly centred on the rival towns of Weymouth and Melcombe Regis, set at Sandsfoot Castle.

In 1869, the 28-year-old **Thomas Hardy** came to Weymouth to work in the office of G.R. Crickmay, a Weymouth architect, helping to restore local churches. Hardy lodged at 3 Wooperton St near Westham Bridge. According to Andrew Norman (author of *Thomas Hardy: Behind the Inscrutable Smile*), he 'bathed every morning; and rowed in the bay every evening'. During this time, Hardy started work on his novel *Desperate Remedies*. The story centres on a young man, Owen Graye, who finds lodgings in Budmouth (Weymouth) and takes up the post of assistant to a local architect (sound familiar?). Later, it was Crickmay who sent Hardy to Cornwall to look at St Juliot's Church near Boscastle, where he met his future wife Emma Gifford. Hardy often stayed in Weymouth to gather inspiration for his prose and poetry and Budmouth is referred to in all but four of his novels.

Jane Austen also often used Weymouth in her novels. In *Sense and Sensibility* she has the amiable but silly Mrs Palmer staying with her uncle in the town. In *Mansfield Park* John Yates leaves Weymouth to join a theatrical party and thus meets Tom Bertram. In *Emma* she makes Weymouth the setting for several scenes, including the secret engagement of Jane Fairfax and Frank Churchill.

John Meade Falkner was brought up in Dorchester and Weymouth. In 1898 his classic tale *Moonfleet* was published, based on a local family of smugglers (the Mohunes) who lived in the area for generations. Fleet House, now Moonfleet Manor Hotel, was built by Maximillion Mohune in 1603 and many of the rooms are named after characters in the story. Memorials to the family can be found at the remains of Fleet Church, most of which was washed away in the Great Gale of 1824.

Weymouth and Portland provide the setting for **John Cowper Powys** novel *Weymouth Sands* (1934). Despite living in America, J.C.P. so loved Weymouth that his ashes were scattered on Chesil Beach.

> 'I have never lived there continuously for more than a few months; but all the same, from earliest infancy to the present day I have always been going there so that the place – its Bay, its salt marshes, its old fort, its breakwater, its chalk Downs, its ancient harbour, its 18th century houses, its early Victorian church, and above all its noble expanse of sand – have come to be more dear to me from an accumulation of memories than any other spot in England or anywhere else.'
>
> (*Remembrances, Weymouth Sands*, John Cowper Powys)

The main character in Powys' novel *Weymouth Sands* 'crossed the road and leaving the old King's Statue before him plunged into the town ... he scarce had time to beat down the image of Perdita before he came along the dark warehouses and narrow alleyways and reached the Tap Entrance of the Weeping Woman [the present Ship Inn] ... so close to the harbour's edge that at one moment she [Perdita] thought she could hear the lapping of the water'.

Modern-day author **Mark Vine** has written *The Crabchurch Conspiracy* based on local characters involved in fighting on both sides during the Civil War. He focuses in particular on the much-overlooked Sydenham family.

William Sydenham was second in command to Cromwell, but the Royalists tried to erase his name from history. The story is a fascinating read.

Music

Weymouth's pubs offer a good choice of live music, especially the Duke of Edinburgh, Boot, Fins, Victoria, Red Lion and Golden Lion. The talented clarinet player *Mike Snelling*, who was born in Weymouth, still plays in jazz quartets. Mike played in the All Stars Band which used to bring in a packed house at the Pavilion every Saturday, and more recently he has been on tour with trombonist Chris Barber. After teaching at Tophill School, he now gives music lessons privately. *Splinter* does Queen and Bon Jovi covers and, with semi-professional Little Roger fronting the band, they really get the place rocking. *Replay* covers music from the 50s and 60s. *Crack* goes in for audience participation with their way-out style. During summer, a mobile stage on the beach opposite Alexandra Gardens allows local bands to perform.

A Local Band - The Dolmen

Take a musician who is passionate about our heritage, dresses as a pirate, supports local charities and is an ex-Portlander now living in Weymouth, and you've got modern-day bard Taloch (aka Tony Jameson), leader of local

The Dolmen regularly plays in local pubs. The acoustic Dolmen, an off-shoot of the main band, comprising Taloch, Josh and Chris, play at the Boot Inn on the first Monday of the month.

band *The Dolmen*. The band comprises Tony (composer, lead vocals, acoustic guitar), Keri Pinney (Tony's daughter, flute), Kayleigh Marchant (bass guitar), Josh Elliott (electric guitar, mandolin) and Chris Jones (drums). This piratical Celtic folk rock group has thus far produced 12 albums, most of them based or themed on cultural heritage.

Having read Mark Vine's book *The Crabchurch Conspiracy*, Tony was inspired to make an album based on the story. Every song holds an historical fact, for instance *The Cold Waters of Weymouth Quay* is dedicated to the 260 Irish mercenaries who lost their lives in 'the Black Hole', an area of the old quayside where Hope Square now stands, during the Battle of Weymouth in February 1645. 'You could make a film of it', says Tony. Mark contributed the main lyrics whilst Tony and Josh concentrated on the melody and performance. Mark became a great friend of the band through this work and is now part of *The Dolmen* team, joining them on tour. Professor Ronald Hutton, from Bristol University, the main historian for English Heritage and star of TV's *Time Team* and *Time Watch*, is the country's leading authority on the English Civil War. He endorsed the album and his voice tells the story. The ground floor of Weymouth Old Town Hall has now been renamed the Crabchurch Room, due to the old building being in the thick of the fighting at the time of the Civil War. Tony says:

> '*I like to promote our local heritage and folklore and have supported events there to raise money for the old Hall's refurbishment. Sometimes I get a little political, an instance being when the ancient and unique landscape leading out to Portland Bill was in danger of being quarried. The Dolmen joined forces with local residents and literally drummed up media support, an example being the holding of the mid-summer celebrations on the land. We were joined by many residents and local Morris dancers. Our efforts paid off and helped save the area. I have at times been able to use our influence with the media to draw attention to particular issues of local importance.*
>
> *Aside from the odd political skirmish we also work closely with Captain Steve Howl and his crew of "Poole Buccaneers" (re-enactors). Steve is "Captain" of The Pirates Keep, a gathering of pirate re-enactors performing at different venues throughout the year, narrating stories to the accompaniment of Dolmen music; it's a concept that explores as well as relives the golden age of piracy. Steve is also one of the narrators on our Storm album. Our music is popular in Europe and this year we're playing at the "Highland Games" in Henk on the Dutch/ German border. It's a great opportunity to embrace the Celtic experience, so I'll be wearing full kilt. Some years ago I got interested in the ancient kilts and now I manufacture them. I guess with my music and re-enactment it qualifies me as an eccentric historian!*'

Dance and Drama

There are several dance schools in the town. *Julie Storey* runs classes every night of the week for different ages, supplies children for the pantomime each year and produces several shows at the Pavilion. All the dance schools around Weymouth get involved. *Juno Belly Dancers* put on a show once a year at Weymouth College and charity shows at other times.

Members of *WOW* (Weymouth's youth theatre group) produce two shows a year at the Pavilion, usually musicals. Tickets always sell out and every year one or two of the cast go on to perform in the West End, they are that good.

Weymouth Drama Club is an amateur dramatics organisation. Adults, young adults and children's groups put on musicals, comedies and plays at the Warehouse Theatre (the club's own intimate studio theatre in Hope St) and the Pavilion. In 2011 they performed *The Tempest* at Nothe Fort in association with the Royal Shakespeare Company. They also organise workshops and social events. Tuesdays are club nights at the Warehouse.

Filming – on Location in and Around Weymouth

The town and surrounding area have been used as a location for numerous films, TV programmes/episodes and videos. Visit-Weymouth.tv has previews and further information.

- *The Dam Busters* (1954), a story of the destruction of the Ruhr dams in 1943 by Barnes Wallis's bouncing bombs – features scenes around the Fleet.
- The harbour was the setting for scenes in Richard Attenborough's film *The Ship that Died of Shame* (1955).
- The Hammer movie *The Damned* (1961) starring Oliver Reed and Shirley Anne Field was filmed on location in Weymouth, with scenes involving the Jubilee Clock and King's Statue.
- Weymouth Bay was used as a substitute for the North Sea in the 1965 war film *The Heroes of Telemark* starring Kirk Douglas.
- *Far From the Madding Crowd* starring Julie Christie and Alan Bates (1967) – scenes were shot on Weymouth Beach and on the hill above Sutton Poyntz (the circus scene).
- Many of the outdoor scenes from the classic 1970s series *The Goodies* were filmed in and around Weymouth and Portland.
- *The Boat that Rocks*, a comedy film based on pirate radio (2008) – filming took place on the former Dutch hospital ship *Timor Challenger*, previously *De Hoop*, moored in Portland Harbour.
- An episode of *Eastenders* (2008) – Barbara Windsor, Samantha Janus, Rita

Simons and Robert Kazinsky spent 5 days shooting scenes on the beach and along the harbourside. Originally planned to film in Spain, cost cutting meant the scenes were shot instead in Dorset.

- Hugh Fearnley-Whittingstall filmed an episode of the *River Cottage* series here. The programme features Hugh kayaking along the coast, fishing and diving.
- Chef Marco Pierre-White visited Weymouth to film an episode of *Marco's Great British Feast*.
- Chris de Burgh spent several days shooting a documentary to accompany his album *Moonfleet and Other Stories* at Wyke Regis, Moonfleet Manor, Chesil Beach, Winspit Caves, the Square and Compass at Worth Matravers, Salterns Marina in Poole and around Purbeck.
- *Nuzzle and Scratch* on CBeebies – features the beach and harbour.
- *Gigglebiz*, another CBeebies show – filmed on Weymouth Beach and at Bowleaze Cove.

Jacqui Gisborne is the Communications Manager at Weymouth and Portland Borough Council. She says: 'Weymouth and Portland's preparation as a "film friendly" location is building and we are seeing production companies returning for further projects.'

Folklore

There have been many reports over the years of strange sightings in and around Weymouth. Some of what follows is gathered from the book *Dark Dorset* and Dave Allan's *Haunted Harbour Tour* is a great way to experience the atmosphere and dark places of the old town. Thanks to Dave for supplying some of the ghost stories.

Strange purple lights and circles of lights in the sky have been seen in Radipole and Littlemoor. A local woman described seeing a pulsating sphere while driving up Ridgeway Hill, and weird lights and other sightings are often reported over the Ridgeway, which is after all an ancient trackway with many barrows. Mysterious flying objects have also been spotted along Portland Beach Road and at Bowleaze.

Crop circles sometimes appear in fields by the Ridgeway near Bincombe. The Bincombe Bumps (six round burial chambers on Bincombe Hill) are known locally as music barrows, as it is said that 'if the ear is laid close to the apex at midday the sweetest melody will be heard within' (*Celtic Tumuli of Dorset* 1866). A more sinister story is that people can be lured to a sleep from which they never awaken, their souls stolen to the Underworld. Smugglers used to say the barrows were haunted to keep people away from their stashes of booty hidden here. Barrow Rise in Wyke Regis marks the spot of another ancient burial site which was destroyed to make way for anti-aircraft guns and later houses. Apparitions have been seen entering the houses here. There is also a spirit road from All Saints Church across Barrow Rise down into the Fleet. A phantom army of Roman soldiers singing in Latin walks the Roman road between Weymouth and Dorchester:

> Visioning on the vacant air
> Helmed legionaries, who proudly rear
> The Eagle, as they pace again
> The Roman Road.

> (*The Roman Road*, Thomas Hardy)

Several hotels in old Melcombe Regis are haunted. The Royal Hotel on the sea front is said to have a resident ghost on the fourth floor. Clarence the ghost patrols the Hotel Rex. An electrician working on the top floor of the Fairhaven Hotel was upset by doors banging shut the length of the corridor, and one of the waiters refuses to go onto this floor after being terrified when the doors at either end of the corridor closed on their own.

Local girl Clare Saul once lived above the butcher's shop opposite Argos in St Mary's Street and tells how a poltergeist used to push her brother down the stairs. So when she started working in Argos, she was less perturbed by ghostly disturbances there than other members of staff.

'The stock room has an oppressive feeling, and other staff have seen moving shadows out of the corner of their eye. At night I've often heard things falling off shelves, seen hobby horses moving on their own and felt things blow in my ear. Since the three flats above the stock room were condemned, there's been more activity in the rooms below. Under the store is a massive cellar which goes all the way back to the Wellington Arms. Several years ago, we were having a refurbishment, and an electrician had to go down there. He was a big, northern chap and we'd cordoned off the trapdoor to the cellar so no-one else could get in. There was this huge crash and he came rushing up, as white as a sheet, saying there was a little girl down there. He'd asked her what she was doing, but she'd run off towards the pub and he'd followed her round the corner but she disappeared in front of his eyes. He said there was no way he was going back down there and had to go home, he was so shaken.'

Others have seen the little girl too. The landlady of the Wellington Arms describes how years ago there used to be an open alley between the two shopping streets, with houses and shops fronting it. Behind the wall cladding in the dining room of the pub are the remains of old bread ovens when this part of the building used to be a bakery. A little girl dressed in white has been seen walking through the wall into what used to be this alley.

Nothe Fort is haunted by a ghost named Gunter, the 'Whistling Gunner', who prowls the underground passageways. Poor Gunter was an artilleryman who, after enjoying one too many tipples, fell off the ramparts to his death. Just down the road is the old Quaker burial ground. Here strange white lights (spirit lights) are often detected when photographing the gardens at night. A story goes that two young Hussars living in the Red Barracks next door, homesick for Hanover, saw a glowing blue light here and thought it was a sign to lead them home. They stole a small boat and set off, but were picked up by an English cutter. Guilty of desertion, they were shot and buried in an unmarked grave here. Thomas Hardy was so moved by their story that he wrote a short tragedy based on their story:

'… the two condemned men were blindfolded, and each placed kneeling on his coffin; a few minutes pause was now given, while they prayed. A firing-party of twenty-four men stood ready with levelled carbines … The two victims fell, one upon his face across his coffin, the other backwards. … Their graves were dug at the back of the little church, near the wall. There is no memorial to mark the spot ….'

(*The Melancholy Hussar of the German Legion*, 1889, Thomas Hardy)

Dave Allan's Haunted Harbour Tour visits the old Quaker burial ground.

Spectral lights have also been seen in Newstead Road Cemetery: 'In the summer of 1991, a Mr Sidney Higgins of Weymouth witnessed a Corpse Candle (a kind of will o' the wisp), while taking a shortcut through the cemetery. He described it as looking like a star as it flittered swiftly past him' (Newland and North 2007).

The ghost of a small Victorian boy haunts Hill Lane near Hope Square. The sad tale goes that he had been tasked with moving barrels but got trapped by them, and despite crying out all night was found dead the next morning.

Children visiting the old Tudor House in Trinity Street have often told of a lady upstairs who speaks to them. In reality there is only Annie, a mute mannequin, seated beside an old bed, but the ghostly nanny tells them all about the bed, which has a rope base and would have been tightened when the children lay down to sleep (hence the phrase 'Sleep tight'). Further down are the Old Rooms. The ghost of a young woman is often seen here, moving through the wall from the pub behind. She attends an old gentleman seated in the window on the top floor of the Old Rooms. The owners of this old house are so used to these apparitions, they simply leave them to it.

Perhaps the *creme de la creme* of haunted places is the Boot Inn, Weymouth's oldest pub. There has been an alehouse on this site since 1346 and over the years landlords have been bothered by ghosts clumping about at night singing sea shanties, locks being tampered with, doors opening and closing at will and glasses flying off the counter. The apparition of a seaman has been seen in the cellar, as well as spectres playing darts – 'one throwing the darts, the other chalking up the score!' (Newland and North 2007, p.93). More recently, there have been sightings of a phantom coachman in the yard outside. Another

The Boot has had many landlords over the years; those who at first did not believe in ghosts have soon been convinced of their existence!

ghost, 'a lady of easy virtue', is said to frequent the dark corner of the pub, waiting for her lost lover. A woman seated here with her dog on its lead felt something behind her but on turning round found nothing, yet the dog's lead had been unclipped by an unseen hand. She promptly left in a hurry.

Opposite the Boot is the Old Town Hall. A spirit has been felt in this old building, parts of which harbour some distinct cold spots. Also in Love Lane behind the Hall 'two ladies in pretty bonnets' have been seen. In one of the terraced cottages here, tenants were unable to account for the smell of rotting meat, which twice coincided with the packing of boxes prior to moving, and strange sightings of a long-nosed figure, described as 'Gonzo' (from *The Muppets*). During the Plague, infected people were boarded up in their homes in an effort to contain the infection, and a person with a long mask stuffed with herbs would visit later to take the dead away. So perhaps the inmates never left. At the end of Love Lane is Franchise Street; this would have seen a lot of military action in the past. People often remark on the strange smell of rotten eggs (gunpowder) and the glistening road surface.

In Melcombe, the Black Dog Inn (even older than the Boot) has resident spooks. An old boy with a trilby hat and pipe frequents the living quarters upstairs, the ghost of a former landlord who can't seem to bring himself to leave. The present barman Martin tells how books have flown off the shelf behind the bar across the room. Pete, the landlord, has heard crashes on the top floor, but on investigating has found nothing out of place, yet the crash has been forceful enough to make a ceiling light swing downstairs. He has also heard footsteps on the stairs and experienced strange, unexplained smells – paraffin, cigars, cooking and candle wax.

In October 1752, a sea monster was washed up on Weymouth sands. It was described as 50 ft long and 12 ft wide, its tongue like a feather bed and mouth wide enough to swallow a coach and horses. When it died and was cut open, thousands of fish leapt out, and people came from miles around to wonder at it.

In July 2010, another monster was found on the sands. Fifty metres long and 5 ft high, this one was created by hundreds of students as part of a sand-

A monster in the sand. (Courtesy of Dorset Echo and photographer Graham Hunt.

sculpting project to raise money for charity. After a JCB ploughed up the sand, students got to work creating the monster. Weymouth sand sculptor Mark Anderson sculpted the head.

Weymouth is also a hotspot for big cat sightings. Merrily Harpur, in *Roaring Dorset! Encounters with Big Cats*, describes ten eye-witness accounts of big cat sightings in and around Weymouth – in Nothe Gardens, at Chafey's roundabout, Westham Bridge, Benville and Chickerell Roads, Station Road, Radipole Lake and Littlemoor. Below is an extract from the book:

'30 January 2007: Shirley Farrar was walking in the woods at Littlemoor at about 2.30 pm when she encountered a "pure black big cat" only 30 ft away, and watched it for 20 seconds. She said: "It was as big as my Doberman, I would say roughly 3 ft tall, including the tail about 5 or 6 ft long. The tail was long and carried low. I was walking my two dogs through woods when they flushed it out and gave chase. The dogs were going crazy and were very unsettled and edgy when they came back. I have also over the last 4 weeks found three deer carcasses completely stripped of all flesh; the last kill was only a day after the sighting."'

Family Fun and Other Activities

Lodmoor Country Park

Just east of the town centre is Lodmoor, a recreational area that has a lot going for it. The Brewers Fayre Restaurant is great for families, with its indoor play area ideal for a rainy day. The Pirate Adventure Golf and Sea Life Park are obvious attractions. The Leisureranch has go-karts and a big slide, and behind it are Sand World, water walkers and a miniature railway. To the rear of the car park is a grassy area leading to the RSPB Reserve, somewhere to walk the dog, kick a ball or enjoy a picnic or barbecue. Just beyond the beautifully kept pitch and putt golf course is a wooden play area and fitness apparatus. Paths lead off from here into the nature reserve.

Sand World

Sand World was created in 2011 by Mark Anderson and friend David Hicks. It provides a unique exhibition space, somewhere to have a go at sand modelling, workshops and special events throughout the year, including an

annual international sand sculpting competition, which adds a real 'wow' factor. From the indoor café you can sit and admire the creations. Mark explains how it works:

Each sand sculpture is crafted by an individual artist, with boards giving information about the sculptors and explaining their inspiration and methods. 'It's good for people to be up close and able to appreciate the sculptures,' says creator Mark.

'Before the sculptor can start, we have to get the sand into a good solid form. This process can take six men 2 weeks. We mix the sand with water into wooden formwork, then use a vibrating trench wacker to compact the sand. When the artists start, they typically expose the top 1.2 m, then carve from the top down, using the formwork below as a scaffold to stand on. The idea for the formworks came from the World Championships in Canada in 1993 when I saw these hugely

impressive sculptures. At Sand World I want to provide a place to showcase the best sand sculptors in the world.'

Miniature Railway and Water Walkers

Darren Melhuish was operating the Water Walkers when the miniature railway business opposite came up for sale in 2008. He invested much time and enthusiasm renovating the railway, and now around 40,000 people a year come to enjoy a ride round the track – mostly families, but also enthusiasts, school groups and disability groups with carers. It's a half-mile (800-m) circuit round the park, with Darren or Roy at the controls. The small shop sells teas, ice creams, picnic things and souvenirs. The 1947 Ferguson tractor is just for show, for the kids to jump on and have a picture taken. Darren says, 'It's a beautiful spot and a lot of locals don't even know we're here. Keeping the park looking nice and litter-free is a job in itself; the rabbits are a particular nuisance as they undermine the track.'

Pitch and Putt Golf Course

Tricia and Ray Bishop took over the pitch and putt course in 2010 and have turned it into a cracking 9-hole course, with bunkers and quality greens. It is an ideal beginner's course, the longest hole being 102 yards. To look really professional, trolleys with six golf balls, a set of irons and brollie are available for just £1 extra. There is also a children's putting green, with clubs provided.

Darren and his Rio Grande 1890 Severn Lamb mock-steam Perkins diesel engine. The single engine and carriages run on a 10¼ gauge track which takes up to 45 people at a time (including dogs).

The course is set in 13 acres (5.3 ha) with trees and sand bunkers. It's a peaceful nature area and wildlife is encouraged, with bird boxes and a bird table.

Tricia serves snacks and drinks from the kiosk and cyclists and walkers are welcome to drop in; the picnic tables under the shelter are a good spot from which to enjoy the view. Dogs can go round the course on a lead. The course is open 7 days a week and yearly membership is available.

Leisureranch

Martin Panrucker and family have run the Leisureranch since 1982, providing Formula K Go-Karts, Cresta Run giant slide, kiddie rides and mini cars for the kids. You have to be above a certain height (4 ft 9 in) to be at the wheel of a go-kart, although little children can be a passenger with an adult driving. On the Cresta Run you can slide for as long as you like, the price is for all day, and little ones can sit on free with an adult. It's great value and families can have hours of fun. The Ranch is open 10 am till 7 pm 7 days a week during the main season and at various times off-peak, though closes in wet weather.

Gardens and Play Areas

- **Sluice Gardens, Lodmoor** – just along the Esplanade from where the land train sets off is a safe area for young children, with sandpit and paddling pool.
- **Greenhill Gardens** – has an 18-hole putting green and tennis courts. It is a popular venue for events (see the notice-board on the hut at the far end of the gardens).
- **Princess of Wales Gardens, Radipole Park Drive** – sometimes referred to as 'the hidden gardens of Weymouth'. Adjacent are tennis and basketball courts, a playground and field, skate park, junior football pitch and multi-use games area. Parking is free for park users. A Friends group helps look after the park and organises fun events such as picnics, musical afternoons and quiz nights.
- **Chapelhay Community Playgarden, Franchise St** – locals meet on the first Sunday of the month (11.30–12.30) for gardening, odd jobs, chatting and playing. There are many planned events – from planting potatoes to Easter extravaganzas.
- **Wyke Gardens, Wyke Rd** – has a tennis court, play area for under 8s and kick-about area for older children. Locals look after the gardens.
- **Louviers Road, Littlemoor** – has a state-of-the-art play area and multi-use games area.
- **Nothe Gardens and Newton's Cove** – great places for rock-pooling and picnics, with views of Portland. See Walks 4 and 5.
- **Sandsfoot Gardens, Old Castle Road** – a small garden, pond full of fish and terraced cafe, backed by Sandsfoot Castle and views of Portland.
- **Jolly Ollie's Adventure Playground, The New Vic, 43 The Esplanade** – children can use the two-storey adventure play area while parents enjoy a meal or coffee. Suitable for 2–10 year olds.
- **Sharkys Soft Play Area and Laser Zone, 9 Custom House Quay** – one of the largest indoor play areas along the south coast. Built around 1840, this old warehouse building has been given a new lease of life. Grown-ups can relax on comfy sofas and enjoy free WiFi connection, while the kids let off steam. There is a separate play area for under 5s.
- **Granby Fun Factory, Granby Industrial Estate** – indoor soft play centre for ages 0–11, with a restaurant and party rooms.
- **Jordan Hill above Bowleaze Cove** – this grassy area used to be a pitch and putt before a local couple bequeathed it to the people, only stipulating that the council keep the grass short and leave the open space for people to enjoy.

Jordan Hill is a top spot for kite flying and popular with dog walkers. It has great views of the bay and free on-street parking. The Lookout Café atop the hill was once the 19th hole on the pitch and putt course.

Leisure Centres

- Weymouth and Portland Swimming Pool and Gym, Knightsdale Road
- Budmouth Community Sports Centre, Chickerell Road
- Redlands Community Sports Hub, Weymouth College, Cranford Avenue

Geocaching

Geocaching is an outdoor treasure hunt using GPS devices to locate containers (geocaches). www.geocaching.com lists an impressive number of local caches, with names like Radipole Walk, Wey Valley Walk, St Mary's Church, Abbotsbury Branch, Upwey, Lodmoor, Town Circuit, Chickerell, Wey Anchor, Coombe Valley, The Hairpin, Portland View, Castle Treasure, Town Bridge, The Crabchurch Conspiracy, Newton's Road Footbridge, Fleet Walk, Westhill Watch, Gone Oyster Catching, Bats and Brewers, and Lookout. Unfortunately, treasure hunters, it isn't possible to reproduce an example cache from the website to whet your appetite owing to copyright restrictions, so you'll just have to search the website yourself.

Guided Tours and Re-enactments

The Pike and Shot Tour and Events Company (www.pikeandshot.com) run by Dave Allan offers a programme of weekly tours between April and October. Contact Dave on 01305 855817 or the TIC for details.

- **Haunted Harbour** – as darkness falls, gather at the Boot Inn, High West Street, for a guided 2-hour walk of old haunts (not suitable for under 10s).
- **Tudor History** – a look back at 16th-century England. The basic walking tour starts from Brewers Quay car park, goes round the harbourside and visits the Tudor House. The half-day tour includes a trip to Portland Castle.
- **English Civil War** – take a boat trip to discover the plot to retake control of the harbour, and learn about the siege and battle for Weymouth and Melcombe Regis in 1645. Includes a visit to Portland Castle and Sandsfoot Castle.
- **Victorian Coastal Defences** – a full day tour taking in Nothe Fort, the Verne Citadel on Portland and other military sites.
- **Smuggling** – a guided walk around the town's smuggling haunts.
- **Portland Roads** – walk from the Nothe, along Rodwell Trail, finishing at Portland Castle. Includes a history of the harbour.

Dave is one of the re-enactors (seen here commenting and covering his ears) at the annual Sandsfoot Castle Tudor Picnic.

Dave started the Pike and Shot business in 2002:

'My wife comes from Weymouth and we settled here when we got married. I set up as a sole trader as an extension to my hobby – historical re-enactments. Every year we re-enact events of the Civil War, including the march of the Royalists from Portland to Weymouth, ending up at the Old Town Hall. The business has

grown over the years, now incorporating shows including the International Living History Fair (held near Leicester, a big indoor trade fair) and the International Napoleonic Fair, both of which I own and run.

In 2010 we became a limited company. I'm the Director but also wash the floors and empty the bin. During winter I do research and planning. I hire people to present different bits and pieces and have a special team for national events. I use local people for the local tours, and the portfolio is always expanding. The tours are designed for locals and visitors, adding to the attractions of Weymouth, and I also go into schools. I've worked closely with the Old Town Hall restoration team and help the Friends of Rodwell Trail with their Tudor Picnic at Sandsfoot Castle. Diversity is the name of the game, trying to develop all the historical links, working with and for people. I'm open to suggestions, and offer advice for people running their own events and can place people with them. I've always had an interest in the past, in understanding history and researching. Often you discover inaccuracies – 'Victorianised' (romanticised) history, wrong perceptions. History is always evolving.'

The Old Town Hall

In September 2009 the Chapelhay Community Partnership (CCP) made securing the future of Weymouth's Old Town Hall its main priority. The project, spearheaded by Martin Hedley, ambitiously took over the lease of the Old Town Hall, paying the council a peppercorn rent in exchange for renovating the building. Using skills within their community and funding from local people and businesses (they receive no external funding), the building is being carefully restored. As Martin explains, the challenge is to organise everyone and plan the work:

'No one is paid, we're all volunteers, for example the architectural metal workers, electricians and architect (Mowlem Metalcraft, A1 Building Services and W4 Projects) have all freely given their services. It's particularly satisfying engaging with people who are normally excluded from working, such as those with mental health disabilities. Everyone has different backgrounds and yet we seem to be able to work as a team and support each other. It's really inspiring and just shows that, supported correctly, such people can be a massive asset to society, not a drain.

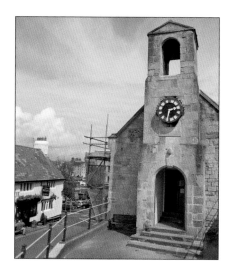

The council has granted us a 30-year lease and has valued our refurbishing work at £140,000.'

The CCP formed a Community Interest Company (CIC) called 'Guardians of the Old Town Hall' to make the project work and part of the 'deal' was that the project has to support the community. So it is more than just a building – it's a focal point. The CIC has created a unique space for people to enjoy local arts, culture, heritage and other community activities. A regular Djembe Drumming Circle and Stitch 'n' Bitch get-togethers are held (where people bring their own craft or learn a new one, over coffee and cake). See the notice-board and website (www.weymoutholdtownhall.co.uk) for other events.

Tudor House

Formerly the home of the Crocker family in the 1860s, Tudor House on Trinity Street now belongs to the Civic Society. It is run as a charity with a band of volunteers who give guided tours (see www.weymouthcivicsociety.org for opening times). Inside is a marvellous recreation of how an early 17th-century middle-class family might have lived. Local architect Wamsley Lewis bought the property before WWII and renovated it; he sourced the furniture from county sales, etc. and willed everything to the Civic Society. Near the fireplace are some old photos of Mrs Crocker and her two daughters: 'They like to still keep an eye on things!' remarks Ann Saunders, one of the Wednesday volunteers.

Other Places to Hang Out

- **Cineworld, New Bond St** – the only cinema in town, with nine screens.
- **Lakeside Superbowl, St Nicholas Street** – 18 lanes, American pool, amusements, bar and diner.
- **'The Front' Skate Park, Preston Beach Road, Lodmoor** – different areas of the park offer different challenges and require varying levels of skill, including an area for beginners. Under 8s should be accompanied by an

adult. Some skateboards and rollerblades are available for hire. Membership is very reasonable and young people can volunteer to help out in exchange for free use of the ramps.

- **Weymouth Baptist Church, 18 The Esplanade** – runs various youth clubs for all ages (tel 01305 787778).

There are also various units that are part of the Youth and Community Service:

- **REVOLUTIONS, 29 St Thomas Street** (tel 01305 778462) – youth workers help young people train and find work. They offer a drop-in centre at weekends and a computer room.
- **STEPS Club, 110 Chickerell Rd** (tel 01305 771861) – youth centre offering recreational activities as well as opportunities to gain qualifications and talk to adults.
- **TIDES Young Persons Project Centre, 2 Newstead Rd** (tel 01305 780563, www.dorsetyouth.org.uk/tides) – aims to teach basic skills and offers help finding employment. They have a music studio, garage for motor mechanics, IT facilities, sport, health and fitness opportunities and a quiet room for chats; they offer group work sessions, help for young mums-to-be, opportunities for accreditation and qualifications and a job vacancies board.
- **WAVES Project, 52 St Mary Street** (tel 01305 768768) – offers advice and guidance to children and young people up to age 20. They work with young people in a variety of ways, keeping those who may be at risk safe from harm, and helping with relationship difficulties, problems at home, bullying, drug and alcohol issues, applying for benefits and finding safe accommodation. They provide access to a shower, washing machine, telephone and internet, a small coffee bar and somewhere to talk to social advisors.

Ron Pryce has been a youth worker for 33 years and is the Senior Project Worker at TIDES:

'*A couple of us used to work at WAVES and realised people kept coming back –something was missing. So we decided what was needed was a project centre. Young people from WAVES drew up what they wanted the centre to be like, what facilities – somewhere to play music, a lounge area, cheap food, cooking facilities, computers, help with practical/mechanical projects. They worked alongside the chippies, electricians, etc. in making the centre, and some of them still come back to see how we're doing!*

TIDES helps young people who may be faced with challenging circumstances, or who aren't sure what they want to do in the future. We help them realise their opportunities and gain new skills. Projects include Employability (CVs, presentation, interview skills), Volunteering, Arts, Personal Effectiveness and Parenting. Projects can be slanted towards what they are already doing. We work with the Adult Education Centre which provides literacy and numeracy courses. Our outreach team goes out on the streets in the evenings to act as a referral point, encouraging young people to drop in and see what we do. We run activities in town so that most people know us.

We also organise trips, e.g. 'Round the World' London, where we visit the Asian neighbourhood of Southall, have an Asian meal, then to multicultural Camden and Chinatown. Weymouth and Portland are very white working class, and some young people haven't been out of their home area and don't get to mix with other nationalities. Also, it's difficult for young people here to find continuous full-time work as a lot of jobs are seasonal, so they may have to travel to get work, and for those who have been brought up here, other places can seem very 'foreign'.

We always need more volunteers – to help with something as simple as making the tea, or just to offer their time, someone to sit and talk to. We also need people with qualifications in psychology and/or who are practically skilled.'

Terry Hawker, Project Worker, runs the garage project at TIDES: 'We could always do with donated stuff like bikes and trailers to work on, woodworking tools, and seeds and plants for the allotment. The other day we had a Role Reversal session. It only lasted about an hour and it was exhausting "playing up" for the kids, but I think it really helped them appreciate some of the things we have to deal with! It's very satisfying working with these young people, helping to turn them around.'

Natasha was referred to TIDES when she was 16:

'I didn't know what I wanted to do, so I took part in lots of projects, including two Dorset awards for Art and one Working with Others. Four of us signed up for the Tall Ships experience and we had to do our own fundraising for it. I'm now doing Health and Social Care at Weymouth College, with work placement here, as I've decided I want to be a youth worker. TIDES helped me grow up and gain confidence; also they've helped me personally, like with moving house. I feel welcome here, I can come and use the computer, chat – it's like my

Natasha and Robert in the kitchen at TIDES.

second home. You can trust the staff and everyone gets along, even though we're all so different. It's not a school atmosphere, it's laid back; they support you to do what you want to do.'

Dog-Friendly Places

Dogs are allowed on the main beaches (Weymouth, Greenhill and parts of Preston beaches) out of season between 1 October and 30 April. Moreover, there are special areas at the Pavilion end of Weymouth Beach and on Preston Beach where dogs may run free at any time of the year.

Watch the signs at the Nothe, as you could be fined if a dog warden catches your dog off the lead. There is a dedicated Dog Exercise Park on Bincleaves Road overlooking Newton's Cove. Dogs are allowed off the lead along Rodwell Trail, though it can be busy with walkers and cyclists. The open grassland on the cliff-top at Bowleaze is a popular dog-walking spot, as well as Lodmoor and Radipole nature reserves.

The Doggie Shop in Maiden Street sells loose feed (ideal for visitors needing a top-up). It offers free delivery and also pet minders, and advertises local animals for rehoming. Alison started the business in 1994 and the photo wall of grateful pets is testament to her friendly shop.

Regular Events

Below is a selection of the many regular events that take place in Weymouth, organised by month. Check with the TIC for exact dates and what is running, as some events may slip into other months. Tel 01305 785747 or visit www. visitweymouth.co.uk.

March

Best of Dorset Leisure Show at the Pavilion
Quad Bike Racing on the beach

April

British Heart Foundation 'Great Parks Charity Walk' – three walks to choose from: an 8-mile (12.9 km), 3.5-mile (5.6 km) and Toddler Trail around Weymouth's parks

May

Beach Kite Festival and Fireworks along the seafront
Harley Davidson Parade and Bike Show at Lodmoor Country Park
'Beat the Gig' Pirate Fun Run, leaving from the Jubilee Clock
Vintage Motorcycle Run, starting and finishing on the seafront
D-Day Vintage and Classic Rally on the seafront
Mad Hatters Tea Party in Greenhill Gardens

June

Folk Festival, set around the old harbour. Morris dancers come from all over the county and bands perform outdoors in Hope Square and in the pubs
D-Day Anniversary Weekend and Picnic at Nothe Fort and Gardens
Armed Forces Day, with parades, bands, convoys, flag ship event, veterans' rendezvous and theatre shows
Classics on the Prom – vintage vehicle rally along the seafront
Skandia Sail for Gold Regatta at the National Sailing Academy

July

Spirit of the Sea Maritime Festival, including the Seafood Festival, Henri-Lloyd Sailing Regatta, Maritime Modelling Festival, Gig Racing Regatta, Beach Live (a series of live concerts on the beach) and water-sports taster sessions both on and in the water.
Weymouth Lifeboat Week on the harbourside
RAF Careers Beach Volleyball Classic (filmed by Sky TV) on the beach
Tudor Picnic in Sandsfoot Gardens

The Spirit of the Sea is a 9-day extravaganza of maritime-related events including the Seafood Festival, which takes place along both sides of the harbour.

August

Fireworks and entertainment throughout August along the seafront
British Heart Foundation Bay Swim
RAF Town Show on the seafront
Victorian Fayre at Nothe Fort
Weldmar Hospice Midnight Walk along the seafront
Dragon Boat Racing in the bay
Weymouth Carnival and Air Show

September

Artwey events throughout the borough
Circus at Lodmoor Country Park
Classic Triathlon

October

Octoberfest at Brewers Quay, with over 50 ales to try
Weymouth Speed Week at the Sailing Academy
Lions Club Beach Motocross
Halloween Festival of Fun at Brewers Quay
Weymouth 10 – 10-mile (16-km) road race along the seafront
Pumpkins in the Park at Greenhill Gardens

November

Community Guy Fawkes Night on the beach
Remembrance Sunday Commemoration at the cenotaphs on the seafront
Christmas Lights Switch On in the town centre

December

Christmas Sparkle – shops stay open till late and there are stalls, outdoor music, carol singing, stars of the panto frolicking with the crowd, etc. The Harbour Traders Association encourages resident boat owners to illuminate their vessels during Christmas
Lions Club Christmas Day Swim in the harbour
New Year's Eve – a good-humoured family event, with people in fancy dress wandering the streets between Hope Square and the Jubilee Clock
Christmas Pudding Race on Weymouth Sands – a charity, fancy-dress event, supported by the RAF. Puddings are given to all runners

Exploring

Trinity Terrace (cat alley)

Walk 1: Greenhill and the Esplanade

Start: Lodmoor car park (some free parking in neighbouring roads)
Finish: The King's Statue
Approx. distance: 1.6 km

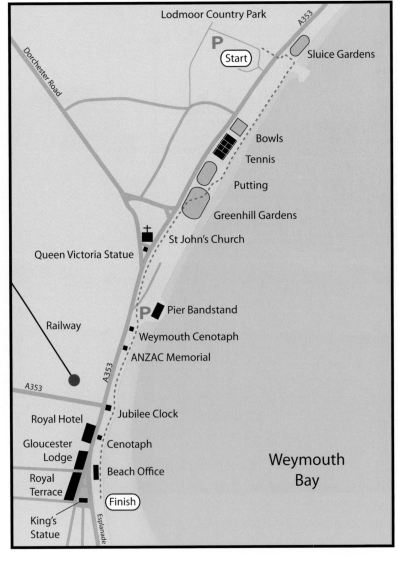

Lodmoor Country Park

A353

P

Start

Sluice Gardens

Dorchester Road

Bowls

Tennis

Putting

Greenhill Gardens

St John's Church

Queen Victoria Statue

P Pier Bandstand

Railway

Weymouth Cenotaph

ANZAC Memorial

A353

A353

Jubilee Clock

Royal Hotel

Cenotaph

Gloucester Lodge

Beach Office

Royal Terrace

Weymouth Bay

Finish

King's Statue

Esplanade

Cross the road and head straight for the beach, signposted Greenhill Gardens. **Sluice Gardens** on the left are so called because they are sited beside a sluice that drains water from Lodmoor into the sea. The beach chalets here were constructed in 1923 as part of a local authority employment scheme, along with relaying the tennis courts, extending the bowling green and landscaping Greenhill Gardens.

Start walking along the Esplanade towards town. Half way along between the two sets of chalets is a flight of steps up to the bowling green, tennis courts and a row of benches, with sweeping views of the bay. Hanging took place on Greenhill, a prime spot for a gibbet! Ahead are **Greenhill Gardens**.

Q Who looks after the wishing well and why?

Q What is special about the lavender, rosemary and curry plants in the flower border?

A The Rotary Club, which collects coins to help local charities.

A They were planted as a sensory garden for the blind, but anyone can enjoy them – try squeezing a leaf or two to release their scent.

The weathervane is a model of the aircraft that held the air-speed record in 1931. Flt Lt George Stainforth AFC was an Old Boy of Weymouth Grammar School (now Weymouth College), an exceptional pilot who set the speed record at 406.92 mph in his Supermarine S.6B aircraft, the forerunner of the Spitfire.

The Armistice Shelter was commissioned by Mayor V.H. Bennett to commemorate the end of WWI. Below the shelter, on the Esplanade, is a mosaic lying resplendent in a former flowerbed. This work of art was supported by local charity the Waterside Community Forum.

Leaving the Gardens behind, walk up to the main road and head towards St John's Church. Constructed of Portland stone with a handsome steeple, this gothic church has some interesting gargoyles.

> **Q** How many strange creatures can you spot (including those round the back of the church), and what are they doing there?

The church was built at the heart of old Melcombe Regis, but it's not much of a centre now, with all the traffic whirring past. In those days, the seafront was the working area and the beach a rubbish dump. Then in the late 1700s, as visitors started to arrive intent on enjoying the benefits of the sea, the Esplanade took shape and began to sport dignified Georgian buildings – first Gloucester Row and Royal Crescent, then Brunswick Terrace, Frederick Place, Waterloo Place and Victoria Terrace. The lovely sweep of buildings shows

A Gargoyles are said to scare off evil or harmful spirits, as well as serving a practical purpose, conveying rainwater away from the building. St John's Church has eight scampering around it.

varying architectural styles – from Georgian red brick and flat facades to stucco-rendered walls with bow windows and later angular bays, now predominantly guesthouses.

Q Who stands looking down the road to Weymouth?

Back on the sea front is the Art Deco **Pier Bandstand**. A pier used to extend into the sea, but the front is all that remains after the seaward end became too costly to maintain. In 1986 two schoolgirls won a national competition to 'press the button' to demolish it. It now houses an amusement arcade, snack bar and restaurant.

Nearby is the **Weymouth Cenotaph** commemorating the dead of both World Wars. In one of the raised stone flower beds, people plant wooden poppies in a mini Garden of Remembrance and it is touching to see all the little flags to 'Dear Granddad'.

Another **stone memorial** here is a reminder of the more than 120,000 Australian and New Zealand Army Corps (ANZAC) soldiers who were repatriated to Weymouth as casualties. In the town's cemeteries are the graves of those who never left. The memorial is situated in front of the Prince Regent Hotel, formerly the Burdon Hotel which was the military hospital in 1915 where many ANZAC soldiers were treated. They were principally sent to convalesce at Montevideo House on Chickerell Road; this was reputed to have been the home of Queen Charlotte, King George III's wife. It was a manor house, later used as a school and then a hospital. A

A Queen Victoria. She and King George III stand at opposing ends of the Esplanade. Some rather chubby dolphinesque creatures guard her plinth.

rare Victoria Regina post box is set in the front wall and an ancient mulberry tree is in the grounds. Road names in Chickerell, Littlemoor and Westham commemorate the sites of other ANZAC camps and convalescent homes, and St Mary's Church in Chickerell has a stained-glass window honouring them. Many local girls became 'war brides' and left for a new life in Australia or New Zealand.

Q Where were these brave soldiers fighting?

Construction of the sea wall began in 1800. On the beach side there were originally 63 metal brackets to hold flags. **Carry on walking along the promenade**. In 1887 the town erected the **Jubilee Clock** in honour of Queen Victoria's 50 years on the throne. One of the panels is a door, allowing access to the working parts of the clock.

Q What is featured on the borough coat of arms above the Queen?

Before the 1920s the Clock stood on the beach and the balconies of the seafront shelters projected over the sand. Then the Esplanade was widened in 1925. The Clock is a focal point on New Year's Eve. Incidentally, look out for pigeons strutting along the Prom. Some may be day trippers from local stud farm Ponderosa UK in Green Lane, Chickerell. Around 2000 racing birds live there and these pigeons are sold all over the world, as far away as New Zealand and Japan.

Just past here is the **Royal Hotel**. When the Old Assembly Rooms became too small for grand balls, a new one was built here. The King often visited as it was a short stroll from his 'Gloucester Lodge'. A red cord separated the royal dancers from the commoners. To the rear were coach-houses, stabling for 60 horses and gardens. When these Rooms became too small, the building was

and castle on the other.

A A three-masted galleon, with three gold lions of England on one flag and a lion

A At Gallipoli, Palestine and on the Western Front.

demolished and rebuilt as a hotel, with the **Royal Arcade** to the right. The public is welcome to use the bar and restaurant and enjoy the entertainment every evening. In the foyer are several striking fireplaces. The foundation stone is set into the Reception desk. The hotel was the American forces' HQ during WWI. The **cenotaph** on the Esplanade opposite commemorates the part the Americans played in the War.

Gloucester Lodge was built in 1780 for Prince William Henry, Duke of Gloucester, the king's brother. It was purchased by King George 21 years later as his holiday residence. Thomas Hardy describes 'the Queen and the princesses at the window' waving to the crowds in *The Trumpet Major*. Servants were 'boarded out' as the Lodge was not large enough to accommodate the entire royal entourage. After the king's death it was extended and became a hotel. It was damaged by fire in 1927 and subsequently rebuilt with an extra storey; the horizontal band of white stone shows the original height of the royal residence. **Royal Terrace** was built *c* 1815 in Gloucester Lodge gardens, originally without shop fronts.

On the sea-side of the beach office (the building on the prom opposite the Royal Hotel) is a stone tablet. What does it commemorate?

'The morning of the 23rd of November, 1824, Melcombe was nearly swept from the face of the earth by a tremendous and terrific hurricane, the wind howled in yelling gusts, the sea roared in a most horrible and frightful manner,

 'Esplanade destroyed by a Tempest Nov 23rd 1824.'

the elements of strife mingled in appalling collision, and nature seemed determined to stamp upon the scene …. The sea broke over the narrows in a strong and dreadful current, two individuals who were at that moment crossing the spot were swept away … whole rows of houses that fronted the foaming, raging, billows, were completely inundated; the pride of Melcombe, its beautiful esplanade, was nearly all demolished, the stone posts and chains … were rent up and entirely broken, the piers … demolished, vessels, boats, and small craft were either driven into the centre of the town, sunk, destroyed, or carried out to sea.

The danger in which the front of the town stood, was appalling, the whole of the roads and streets were covered with the rolling billows, driving impetuously masses of sand and stone, boats were observed floating in close approximation with vehicles of various descriptions, such a scene of devastation and ruin were never remembered to have been observed before; orders were speedily issued for the reparation of the town, the walls were erected in a more secure manner, and soon the scene of destruction was followed by one of perfect security.'

(*The History and Antiquities of the Borough and Town of Weymouth and Melcombe Regis*, 1829, George Ellis, Dorset County Museum)

Cross the road onto the island to look at the King's Statue. The 'Grateful Inhabitants' of Weymouth held a General Meeting 'to consider of the most proper mode of celebrating' the 50th year of the King's reign. It was decided to set up a committee and subscription for relief of poorer Brethren (local families) and fellow Townsmen now Prisoners of War in France. They

commissioned a life-like statue 'as a memorial to future ages of the Virtues of the Monarch and of the Gratitude which this Town feels for having been so frequently honoured by the Royal Presence'. The statue is set on a plinth of Portland stone. The King is dressed in his coronation robes, books of the Constitution of England are on his left, a lion and unicorn at his feet, the whole made of Coade Stone, an artificial material of long-weathering character. The Grade I Listed statue was repaired by local painter Warwick Brown, who spent 7 days just painting the King's face and many more days restoring his heraldic colours.

> **Q** Look to the hills northeast above Weymouth. Can you see another memorial to the King?

A local story tells how the King was annoyed because the carving showed him riding away from Weymouth, yet it was carved 3 years after his last visit to the town, so the King never saw it (which rather puts doubt on the story). Moreover, according to local historian Martin Ball, it shouldn't be white at all, as it is supposed to depict the king on his favourite grey charger. Martin suggests that it faces away from Weymouth because it was a snub by Republican rebels to royal interference. Designer James Hamilton portrays the King with cocked hat and 'unreasonable' spurs (according to Frederick Treves).

To return to Lodmoor, catch a bus from here or stroll back along the Esplanade. Alternatively, you might like to take the seafront land train, which operates between Easter and September.

▲ The white horse and rider on the hill above Preston and Osmington were carved here in 1808 because it was said the King enjoyed riding so much on these hills with his officers. Army engineers were tasked with drawing the outline.

Walk 2: Town Centre and Quayside

Start and finish: The King's Statue
Approx. distance: 3 km (including 1 km loop to Pleasure Pier)

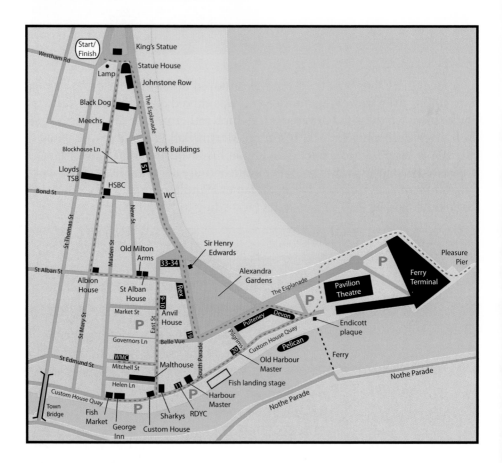

Behind the King's Statue is **Statue House**, little changed from 200 years ago. At one time it was the public library. Together with the adjacent building, it makes an imposing entrance to the main shopping area.

Follow the Esplanade towards the Pavilion. The first set of buildings (**Johnstone Row**) were designed by James Hamilton, the local architect responsible for the King's Statue, Royal Crescent and Gloucester Row. **York Buildings** further on (Nos 53–37) in 1783 were considered to be one of the finest seafront terraces in the country. The house with the three-storey bow windows shows how these houses would have looked originally.

The white painted building with arched windows (**No. 51**) was originally Harvey's Library and Card Assembly, and later the headquarters of the Royal Dorset Yacht Club. The Library provided, apart from books, somewhere to read the papers, play cards, drink tea and shop. Assembly Rooms in the Royal Hotel and Trinity Street were other entertainment venues.

The Renaissance-style building **on the corner of Bond St** was erected in 1883 as Stuckey's Bank. This changed hands but remained a bank until the building was converted to its present use as public conveniences. 'The opportunity to enter a French Chateaux should not be passed over lightly' (Ricketts 1976).

The large building at 90 degrees to the seafront (**Nos 33–34**) used to be the old Pier Bathing Station. Bathing machines operated usually until midday, after which visitors enjoyed leisure pursuits, centred on the library and theatre, which were fairly exclusive institutions.

Standing proudly at the head of Alexandra Gardens is the statue of Sir Henry Edwards. It commemorates his 'public services, munificent charity and private worth'. If the sun is shining on the statue, you may see small silvery flecks of the mineral muscovite in the marble. The plinth is Cornish granite with feldspar crystals. Sir Henry paid for the clock on the Jubilee Clock Tower – a long-awaited public enhancement at a time when ordinary folk did not possess timekeeping devices; also Edwards Avenue on Rodwell Road, Edwards Homes on Rodwell Avenue and the Working Men's Club in Mitchell St. There is another memorial to him in Melcombe Regis Cemetery.

Alexandra Gardens were the town's first public gardens, built on the site of the old town midden (refuse tip). The bandstand here was later enclosed by a miniature crystal palace. This later acted as the reception centre for ANZAC troops arriving in Weymouth, then as a concert hall and amusement arcade, before being destroyed by fire in 1993.

Walk round the back of the Gardens. Pass the end of **St Alban Street**, formerly known as Petticoat Lane (pre 1872), now locally called Flag Street because of its bunting.

The **Hotel Rex** was built in 1795 as the Duke of Clarence's summer residence when the Royals were in town (he was the third son of George III). He later became King William IV. In his youth he served in the Royal Navy and was known to have fathered at least 10 illegitimate children and amassed exorbitant debts before ascending to the throne, hence his nickname of 'the Sailor King'. However, he was a good king and during his reign the Poor Law was updated, child labour restricted and slavery abolished. Dukes Restaurant occupies the original wine cellars. The hotel has a lovely hung staircase.

Q Who is having breakfast in the window of the Beaufort guesthouse?

At the end of this row is an Italian-style house, **No. 19 Clarence Buildings**. This was built as a sanatorium for women and children in 1848. It housed the local authority between 1904 and 1971 and is now holiday flats.

Continue round behind the Gardens. Pulteney Buildings (Nos 7–15) were named after Sir William Pulteney who reclaimed the land here. Both these and **Devonshire Buildings (Nos 1–6)** have a rather uniform look due to local authority enforcement. Houses like these were designed as holiday lodgings rather than homes.

A Big Ted and Little Ted.

Ahead of you is the **Pavilion Theatre and Ferry Terminal.** These were built on land reclaimed in 1908. The Pavilion opened in 1960 with *Let's Make a Night of It* starring Benny Hill. Over the years many people have performed here and gone on to become household names, including Dick Emery, Bruce Forsyth, Bradley Walsh, Joe Pasquale and Billy Pearce. The theatre has been reinvigorated in recent years, thanks to the Working Group, volunteers and supporters. Besides shows, the ballroom is often used for wedding receptions, boxing tournaments, conferences and exhibitions. Reduced price parking is available for those attending a show. The Pavilion Privilege Card gives lots of benefits if you use the Pavilion often, including behind-the-scenes tours.

Ray Banham inspecting the new stage flooring. In November 2010 (the 50th anniversary of the Pavilion), Ray and Julie Storey produced and directed two performances, the profits from which were ploughed back into the Pavilion. As well as a new stage surface, a Tannoy system was installed between the stage and dressing rooms, which should help performers.

To the right of the entrance door is a wall plaque telling how the entire population of Alderney sought refuge in Weymouth in June 1940. The café inside has good views of the bay.

> **Q** Just before the door to the ballroom is a wall of memorabilia to war veterans, who hold regular meetings here and veterans' weekends. Which troops are marching along the Esplanade?

Behind the Pavilion is the **Pleasure Pier**. It opened in 1933 and at a quarter of a mile (400 m) long and 100 ft (30 m) wide it provided three new berths, two rail tracks, each able to accommodate up to 50 wagons or a full-length passenger train, and electric cranes. It's a shade of its former glory, but a popular fishing spot. Take a stroll out to the end if you like.

Leaving the Pavilion behind, **walk towards the harbour**. You can still see the old railway tracks in the road; trains ceased running in 1994. **Go up the steps onto the raised quay**, the start of Custom House Quay. A stone and

A Americans on their way to Normandy. More than 500,000 troops and 144,000 tanks and vehicles left from Weymouth and Portland and thousands of GIs died or were wounded on Omaha Beach alone, fighting to keep the Germans from our shores.

plaque here commemorates John Endicott's sailing from Weymouth and the founding of Salem, Massachusetts, in 1626.

> **Q** What are you reminded of when you look back across to the end of Devonshire Buildings (the terrace of houses you walked past)?

Further on is **Pilgrims Way**, a small street off to the right, which commemorates the many pilgrims who sailed from the port. **No. 20 (Harbour Master)** was originally a merchant's house, its large bay windows allowing the merchant to keep an eye on his shipping interests. It was then used as a customs office until 1985, when the building became the Harbour Master's Office for a time; this later moved down the street. The staging here would have been the centre of a busy scene – with boats moored and cargo being unloaded, some using cranes, parts of which can still be seen here. Today, local fishermen pull up and offload their catch at the staging.

> **Q** There are some interesting door knockers at Nos 14–17. What can you spot?

The current **Harbour Master's Office** is another handsome building, a former grain store. Huge boats carrying up to 6000 tons of corn would draw up at the quayside to offload their grain, which could take a good week to discharge into the town's flour mills. To give these large vessels room to swing across the river, they had to widen the harbour in the 1880s by cutting away the bank opposite. A hoist system would be used to transfer goods from the ships to the top floor of quayside warehouses; then by a series of trapdoors, goods were lowered for storage in allocated rooms until required for delivery to the customer.

No. 11 is an 18th-century building that used to house the public baths. It is built partly of creamy-coloured Bath stone. In 1866 it became the Sailors' Bethel, a Christian institute for seamen. Today the building is home to the **Royal Dorset Yacht Club**.

A A sea dragon, anchor and flip-flop.

A The end house is shaped rather like a lighthouse.

Sharkys, a few doors down, used to be a fish and fertiliser warehouse until 1965.

Custom House is one of Weymouth's best Georgian houses, originally a merchant's elegant abode. The Custom Service used it between 1874 and 1985, then it became the HM Coastguard Portland Maritime Rescue Co-ordination Centre. The Centre co-ordinates distress calls and incidents from the Hampshire/Dorset border to Exmouth, an area of approx. 2000 square miles (5180 km²); 999 calls are received here and staff organise how they are going to co-ordinate the rescue. The wheel and gibbet in the foyer were originally housed on the top floor to hoist goods up from the flat carts in Helen Lane behind.

Ship building used to take place along the quayside, which until 1721 ended at around the **George Inn**. Jack Randbury, an ex-smuggler, used to own the pub. One story goes that he hid in the chimney of the George while Revenue men were chasing him. The old inn dates back to 1665, when its owner, Sir Samuel Mico, a silk merchant, bequeathed it to the town and its profits went to help aged seamen and poor apprentice boys. The charity continues to this day, providing educational grants to young people, supporting apprentices and paying a small pension to 'poor decayed seamen'. Each year there is a special wreath-laying ceremony at St Mary's Church followed by a procession of the trustees of the charity, descendants of Sir Samuel, seaman and young beneficiaries to the quay. The low ceilings in the George Inn together with the open loft space lend character to the inn today.

Q To the right of the George is a wall plaque. Why is this site important in England's history?

To the left is the **Old Fish Market** which dates from 1855 and still sells local fishermen's catches (see the section on 'Local Fare'). The building was constructed with Portland Stone ashlar blocks; some of the weathered surfaces clearly show the fossils of shells, typical of this limestone.

A The Black Death entered England here. The monk William of Malmesbury described its arrival: 'In the year of our lord 1348 … the cruel pestilence, terrible to all future ages, came from parts over the sea to the south coast of England, into a port called Melcombe in Dorsetshire.'

Retrace your steps to Custom House and turn left up East St, leaving the harbour behind. There are several noteworthy buildings in this area. In **Helen Lane** (formerly Hell Lane) is the Old Malthouse. This area used to be where 'gentlemen' would go for a night out with 'the ladies'.

> **Q** What is unusual about two of the windows of the Globe Inn?

The Working Men's Club in Mitchell St is a handsome brick and stone building dating from 1873, built and paid for by Sir Henry Edwards. To the working classes it offered a library, with periodicals and newspapers, a place to eat and drink, enjoy lectures and socialise. Facilities today include darts, pool and skittles, with matches every night of the week during winter. Visitors can apply for temporary membership.

Back on East St, the pedestrian alley left of the car park is known as **Governors Lane**. It got its name from the 'Governor' of Melcombe Regis, Colonel William Sydenham, who put up a brave stand against the Royalists during the Civil War.

> **Q** Anvil House (Nos 9–10) is a handsome brick building with stone-arched windows. It has some interesting carvings — what can you make out?

Turn left into St Alban Street. Evidence of a sand spit and sea shells have been found under the street. Formerly, an abbey stood in this area, the exact site of which is uncertain, though Maiden St, East St and Governors Lane would have formed the boundary. A few small stone walls can be seen, relics of the monks' buildings. Nuns lived round the corner in Maiden St. In the 13th century, monks from Abbotsbury would walk the 7 miles (11.3 km) to Weymouth, along the ancient trackway through Friar Waddon and Upwey, following the River Wey into town. The Dominican monks who lived here were concerned with saving the poor and assisting pilgrims bound for

A They are shaped like portholes.

A A couple of lions holding crosses or keys, shields, ribbons/swags, flowers, fruit and leaves, faded Latin inscriptions, and above some faces peering down.

Santiago di Compostella in Spain to visit the relics of St James.

St Alban House (20 m on the right) used to be a merchant's house in the 1500s and then a school. Evidence of a burial ground has been unearthed across the street.

Next on the right is an old Tudor building.

Q Round the corner there is a plaque on the wall. What does it tell you?

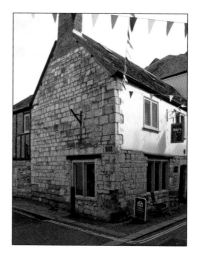

This building has had many uses over the years. It may originally have been a simple, single-storey guest-house for pilgrims. A visiting spiritual medium 'detected' monks walking about in the building, in a place marked by large paving slabs under the floor, possibly the site of an old courtyard. It was damaged in the War, and during restoration skulls were found in the chimney.

Walk on to St Mary's Street, one of the main shopping thoroughfares. On the corner is **Albion House**, a former public inn.

Turn north up St Mary's Street. Keep looking up above the modern-day shop fronts and you'll be able to appreciate the former elegance and grandeur of Weymouth's town centre buildings.

Q In the paving, a round plaque marks something.

A This was once the Milton Arms, Milton Abbey owned the buildings here, hence the name.

A This is the site of the ancient maypole. School children used to gather here on May Day to dance and celebrate.

Bond St used to be an open sewer, an inland sea waterway washing in and out. Take a moment to admire the carvings around the door of the **HSBC Bank**.

Continue down St Mary Street, past Lloyds TSB. **Blockhouse Lane**, a narrow passageway on the right, is named after the Elizabethan fort sited here in 1586. It had five mounted guns facing Weymouth Bay, at the ready should the Armada sail within range.

Messrs Meechs has an interesting frontage, with dragons over the rainwater heads and on the window corners. It may be surprising to know that this romantic Gothic façade was only put up in 1924.

The Black Dog is an old-fashioned beer house with lots of character. It was originally called the Dove but changed its name after a sea captain from Newfoundland gifted 'a great black beast of a dog' to the landlord as thanks for his hospitality. So many people came to see the animal that the landlord

renamed the inn. There used to be four separate drinking rooms with an open walkway through the middle. Ruts have been left in the flagstones by the carts that used to traffic through. In the 'Mess Deck' is a collection of ships' names off sailors' hats, some gold-threaded, and the inn has been adopted by *HMS Portland* as their home pub. Present landlords Pat and Pete Slade are very welcoming:

'When the cellar floor was dug out, flint-lock muskets were found inside a chest; they're in the Museum now. They also discovered two entrances to tunnels, but there were human remains here so they blocked them up again. One was probably an old smugglers route, the other perhaps King George's whoring entrance, when he used to take to the back room with his ladies, while his bodyguards kept watch out front. He frequented the place so much he presented the pub with two royal crests (see the fireplaces). We're technically in Melcombe Regis and older than the Boot in Weymouth, and yes we're haunted. There's a lot of spiritual activity here.'

The Black Dog used to lie inside Melcombe Regis town boundary, and smuggled goods run onto the beach could be sneaked into the inn, then via a system of tunnels to the White Hart. A murder took place in front of one of the fireplaces when two men of the Hawhurst family whipped a fellow smuggler to death in 1758 for letting slip some information; a plaque above the bar tells the story.

At the end of the street you are back at the King's Statue.

Q What is special about the street lamp directly behind the Statue?

A It was presented to the town by the Mayor of Louviers in Normandy, France, to commemorate 30 years of twinning. Weymouth is also twinned with Holzwickede in North Rhine-Westphalia, Germany.

Walk 3: Town Centre and Marina

Start: Frederick Place behind the King's Statue
Finish: The Palm House, Swannery Lake (there is car parking here)
Approx. distance: 2.2 km

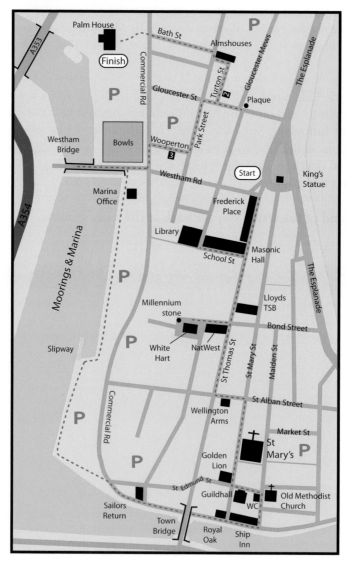

The terraced houses of **Frederick Place** at the start of St Thomas Street were built in 1834 in the gardens of Gloucester Lodge, which extended as far as the Masonic Hall in School Street. William Thompson, a naturalist and the world's first underwater photographer, lived at **No. 11**. He owned two boats, which he used to trawl and dredge Weymouth Bay for specimens. He was an expert on anemones and seaweed, discovering several new species. If it wasn't for him, the rocks beneath Sandsfoot Castle, Byng Cliff and the Nothe would not be populated with Peacocks Tail seaweed. In 1856 he wrote:

'My object in studying photography is in order to illustrate objects of natural history, as I unfortunately cannot use my pencil. ... This application of photography may prove of incalculable benefit to science. We may take (to a reasonable depth) sketches of submarine rocks, piers of bridges, outlines of sand-banks, in fact, everything that is required under water. Should a pier of a bridge require to be examined, you have but to suit your camera, and you will obtain a sketch of the pier, with any dilapidations; and the engineer will thus obtain far better information than he could from any report made by a diver.'
(William Thompson)

Next door is the **Masonic Hall**. This fine 1816 building is based on a Neo-Palladian Grecian temple. Round the corner in **School Street** is the Lodge Room; originally there were windows in the side of the Room, but these were infilled to avoid Window Tax. In 1876 the Hall was extended to include a dining room and Myrtle Cottage. In 2017 the Lodge will celebrate its 250th Anniversary and hopes to create a banner based on its logo – three castles and a square and compasses (the original coat of arms of the Premier Grand Lodge of England formed in 1717) together with the arms of Weymouth and Melcombe Regis granted in 1592 – as depicted in the circle at the top of the Dining Room stained-glass window.

 What Masonic symbols can you identify in the windows?

A   In the bottom left-hand corner are the Square and Compasses. In the right-hand corner are the Square, Level and Plumb Rule. These represent the practical tools used by stonemasons and are used in Freemasonry to teach moral and spiritual values. In the centre is the Seal of Solomon representing the fusion of opposites, with God at the centre of the Universe.

Freemasonry is a society of men that instils in its members a moral and ethical approach to life: it seeks to reinforce thoughtfulness for others, kindness in the community, honesty in business, courtesy in society and fairness in all things. Members are urged to regard the interests of the family as paramount. It teaches and practises concern for people, care for the less fortunate and help for those in need, and its Grand Charity is the largest grant-giving charity after the National Lottery.

Weymouth Library occupies the site of old St Mary's School, hence the name of this street, School Street. A plaque, originally on the school wall and now above the main library stairs, states: 'It is my wish that every poor child in my dominion should be taught to read the Bible (His Highness George III)'. **Return now to St Thomas Street.**

Q A few houses down there is a café with some interesting black and white pictures left and right of the windows. What can you make out?

Lloyds TSB (*c* 1765) and **NatWest** further down the street are both elegant buildings. Banks in the old days were built to impress, to exude an air of solidity and impregnability. Red granite columns flecked with red feldspar, grey transparent quartz and black biotite frame the door of NatWest. A carving of a Herculean/Neptune figure appears to be holding up the rest of the building. The frame of the port-hole-shaped window is beautifully carved, with a screaming face. On the roof a pair of languid figures are reclining.

Turn down **New Bond St**. This street used to be known as Coneygar Ditch, the medieval town's defensive limit. This is where the old Jubilee Hall was sited, Weymouth's answer to entertainment in 1887. Designed by local architect

---

A Two galleons, geese/swans in flight, apples(?) on a tree, a setting sun and flash of lightning, sea creatures (snakes and a crab).

Crickmay, the Hall was *the* place for dancing and theatricals. Moving with the times, it was later used as a cinema, bingo hall and night club. Arcadia on the north side of the Hall was originally an open-air roller skating rink, covered over in 1911 to provide a dance hall. The **Millennium stone** set in the pavement outside Debenhams commemorates the opening of the new retail site in 1989 after Jubilee Hall theatre was dismantled and moved to Poundbury, where it is set to form part of Queen Mother Square. Debenhams mirrors the old theatre.

The **White Hart Tavern** dates back to the 15th century. In 1654 it was the scene of riots against Navy press gangs. It is also the birthplace of the artist Sir James Thornhill (born 1675).

Back on St Thomas Street, continue down and turn left into **St Alban Street**. The **Wellington Arms** is a 16th-century inn with a Grade II Listed frontage. Affectionately known as 'the Wellie', it is popular with locals and holidaymakers, who come back year after year, and is a traditional family-run pub – 'Only one member of staff isn't family, but might as well be', says the landlady. Inside, the walls are covered with old photographs and pictures, including two upside-down frames denoting the number of refurbishments. Like many old pubs in Weymouth, it is haunted.

St Mary's Church is your next stop, **south down St Mary's Street**. In 1299 there was a small chapel here for local fishermen, which existed through to 1604 as a chapel of ease (for the attendance of those who could not reach the parish church conveniently). Then a new church was built. George III worshipped here regularly, but it became unsafe, with bits of ceiling frequently falling during services. In 1815 the old church was demolished and the present Classical-style church replaced it, built of Portland stone ashlar (dressed stone). It has a particularly tall pulpit to allow the rector to keep an eye on folk in the galleries. Inside, above the altar, is a painting of *The Last Supper* by Sir James Thornhill. The curtains give a rather theatrical look. The town's war memorial and book of remembrance are on the north side of the chancel. A cooperative of about 50 locals rents one of the side rooms as an art and craft outlet. A wall plaque in the room here reads rather interestingly to '… one of ye Worst of Men; Friend to ye Distres'd; truly Affect'd; and kind Husband'. The church is open Tuesday mornings for coffee and a chat and there are lunchtime chamber concerts usually once a month. At weekends, street pastors take to the streets at night, supporting the police and ambulance service. On Saturday mornings they set out chairs by the maypole plaque for al fresco worship. The graveyard was deconsecrated many years ago and is now a private car park.

Q Beside the church is a passageway. What is odd about the carvings either side of the door of No. 45?

Continue to the **end of St Mary's Street** where it joins St Edmund Street. On the right is the **Golden Lion**, an 18th-century coaching inn. The London stage coach used to leave Ludgate Hill every day at around 5 am on its 130-mile (209-km), 15-hour journey to Weymouth, stopping at Salisbury, Blandford and Dorchester. Coaches also arrived from Bristol, Bath and Yeovil. The lion above the entrance has had its tail stolen numerous times; in 1945 it was damaged by overexuberant GIs celebrating Victory night by riding the beast. Luckily the landlord now keeps it in good repair.

The large building on the opposite side of the road is the **Guildhall**. Built of fine Portland stone, with its front arcade topped by pillars, it has the air of a Greek temple about it. It was built in 1837 on the site of the medieval Town Hall of Melcombe Regis.

To the east the old **Methodist Church** faces the street and dates from 1866. Stand with your back to the church and look across at the **Jacobean building on the corner**. This was once the town's fire station and is now a public conveniences and RAFA Wings Club.

A The two figures of a man and woman have huge pot-bellies and little hooves. They make a comical pair.

Q What is embedded in the wall of the gable?

Walk down to the Quay and turn right, along the quayside. The **Ship Inn** used to be much smaller but was extended in the 1950s when the old Red Warehouse and fishmongers next door were demolished. Upstairs is a wall mural painted in 1979 by pupils of Blandford Upper School. The inn has been refurbished and offers great views of the harbour. It almost feels like a ship, with the intimate alcoves, candles and lanterns, old leather chairs, panelling and navigational charts papering the walls.

The **Royal Oak** is a friendly traditional pub, with sawdust on the floor and a barrel of unshelled monkey nuts. It's a simple one-room bar with outdoor

A A (replica) cannonball, possibly fired from a Royalist ship in the Black Hole inlet across the harbour. Colonel Sydenham's quarters were behind this building and would have been a prime target during Civil War.

seating and a good selection of ciders. Dogs are welcomed with a jar of biscuits on the counter.

Take the road under the Town Bridge towards the marina. The charter boats moor up here. The middle section of the **Sailors Return** was once a butcher's shop and it was converted in Victorian times into one inn. On the wall inside is a fine 17th-century map of the town. A rope ferry operated here until 1769, when it was abandoned due to the increasing number of boat traffic accidents.

> **Q** What tracks are you following underfoot?

Old warehouses once lined the road here, now replaced in the most part by apartments. For years the Hanney family used to run a crab processing business here. Local crabs were dressed before being packed off to London and the Channel Islands. They were the first in Weymouth to sell frozen food wholesale. **Alongside the marina**, notice how some of the harbour piles extend above the top of the wall; this is so that the paddle-steamers could moor here without risking their paddle boxes overriding the wall during very high tide and becoming caught when the tide dropped.

> **Q** Halfway down the Slipway are some information boards. What must boats obey before entering the port?

The multistorey car park opposite is built over a burial ground (in old Bury St), the principal cemetery for Melcombe Regis when St Mary's churchyard became overcrowded.

Just past the Marina Office is **Westham Bridge**. This was a special building project creating work for the unemployed after WWI. It opened in 1921 to form a tidal barrier to Radipole

A Traffic lights.

A The old Weymouth Harbour Tramway. Imagine trains 'speeding' past at 4 mph, a bell ringing continuously and a man (the shunter-in-charge) whistling and waving a flag and hand lamp to ensure people moved out of the way of the tram.

Lake, which is now freshwater with sluices controlling the water level. In 1973 a parallel footbridge was built and the bridge was closed to traffic in 1987 when the Swannery Bridge was built. Walk to the middle section of the bridge to see the sluice mechanism.

> **Q** A rather unusual building is 'moored' on the Lake. What does it remind you of?

Back on Commercial Road, opposite the bowling green, cross the road and go east down Wooperton St.

> **Q** Which famous author lodged at No. 3?

Turn left, then right into Gloucester Street.

> **Q** What is unusual about the terraced houses on the right?

Up ahead on the corner house is a wall plaque describing how this was once the site of **Gloucester Mews**. The extensive mews had to accommodate all the men, horses and coaches required by the Royals staying in Gloucester Lodge. It later developed into a bus garage, before being converted into a picture house (the Picturedome) in 1933. In the 1970s it showed mainly X-Certificate and uncensored films.

Retrace your steps and turn right into Turton St. The King's mistress was rumoured to live in **Turton Villa (No. 2)**, conveniently situated behind Gloucester Lodge. At the end of the street are some Gothic **almshouses** built *c* 1835 with unusual pointed windows.

Turn right, then left into Bath St and back to Commercial Road. Cross the road and head for the Palm House – an ideal place to end your walk. These historic glasshouses were erected in 1927 and have been renovated by Nigel and Victoria Duff, who have made use of many of the building's original features:

A They have interesting carved figureheads between the door arches.

A Thomas Hardy (1869–71), while apprenticed to the architect G.R. Crickmay. *Desperate Remedies*, his first novel, was largely written here.

A An ark perhaps? This used to be Noah's Ark Aquarium. Later it became an amusement arcade before being converted into a restaurant. It isn't floating at all, but sits on a concrete platform.

'For many years, the building belonged to Weymouth's Parks and Gardens Department and housed the Borough's collection of palms and other exotic plants, including a banana tree. It was the centrepiece of a complex of glasshouses which produced thousands of bedding plants for the seafront borders and other parks and gardens. When we took it over, we metamorphosed it into a contemporary place, keeping the original architecture – the brackets and timber framing (which needs painting once a year) and the old mechanism for opening the roof vents, which still works. We encourage people to stop awhile, enjoy the comfy sofas, and great coffee and tea, and read the newspapers. The outside sun-deck is very popular. Cyclists and walkers with dogs are welcome, as well as children, who can use the play areas. It's all about relaxation.'

The enclosed outdoor sandpit, balance beams, climbing wall, stepping stones and little crooked house are enjoyed by children, while the indoor lounge and play area 'Blooming Kids' for under-5s means that little ones can play freely while parents relax. In another wing is a ceramics studio, where people of any age can have a go at designing pottery to take home. The gift shop sells local art and craft-work, including nautical and garden gifts, wall art and preserves. The Palm House is also available for hire, though it is not licensed. It is open every day from 9.30 am till 4.30/5.30 pm. Battery-powered bicycle hire is available and, as the Palm House is situated at the convergence of many cycle routes, users can explore and enjoy all the cycle-ways available, including the predominantly traffic-free Rodwell Trail. Adjacent is an outdoor playground. The Lake, together with the bird reserve, is home to Weymouth's famous swans and many other interesting birds.

Walk 4: Harbourside and the Nothe

Start and finish: Hope Square (free parking in residential streets around here)
Approx. distance: 2.2 km

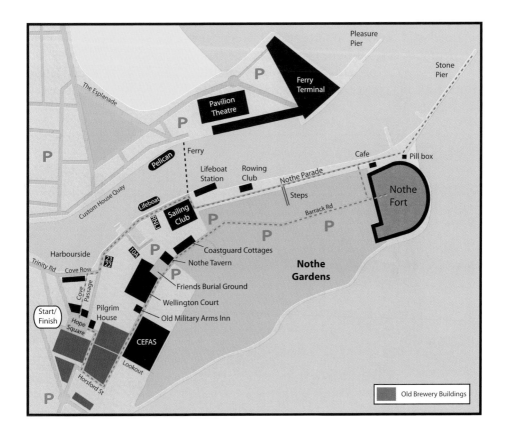

Brewing has taken place in Weymouth since 1256. There was a good freshwater spring at Chapelhay to the west of Brewers Quay and fields of barley in Radipole, so everything needed was close by. The buildings known as Brewers Quay were built in 1903/4 as Hope Brewery for John Groves. Devenish and Davis also set up business here, but the latter went to the wall quickly, leaving

Groves and Devenish to fight it out. During WWII the area was bombed, but the brewery was beautifully repaired using original materials. Groves was bought out by Devenish in 1960, then itself closed in 1985, when all brewing ceased for a period of 10 years. The buildings were adapted for a mix of uses, with some brewery equipment retained and used by micro-brewer Giles Smeath of the Dorset Brewing Company, which continues to brew in the traditional way and is now based in Crossways. The **old brewery and malting buildings around Hope Square** form a conservation area and constitute an unusually intact brewery landscape.

During the first weekend in October there is a beer festival in Hope Square. The Square is built on reclaimed land, the area once being an opening to the sea known as Ope Cove or Black Hole before the land was reclaimed in 1781. Picture water lapping roughly in line with where the Red Lion flower tubs are now and warehouses all along the old waterfront. It was here that several hundred Royalists were trapped on the wrong side of Black Hole and driven into the water to their deaths.

> In the end wall of Pilgrim House (to the right of the post box and bench) is an indentation left by what?.

Narrow **Cove Passage** lies between the Crow's Nest and Red Lion. The tiny nautical antique shop in this alleyway opens on request. Note also the old warehouse on the right. **Head towards the harbourside.** At the end of the passage, to your left are six terraced houses making up **Cove Row**, an early example of town planning, though in recent years there have been many alterations. **Turn right along the harbourside.**

> Be careful not to trip over the large metal rings and shackles here. Can you guess what they are doing here?

A A cannonball. It was probably fired from old Chapelhay Fort above the harbour.

A They used to secure the cross-Channel steamers when they were laid up in the Cove during winter; these rings date back to the 1880s.

No. 22 was formerly the Hope Tavern (notice the bracket for holding the sign).

> **Q** What is odd about No. 23?

Walk along Nothe Parade. Where the bridge crosses the slipway there is an old established shipyard. **No. 10A** is the Slipmaster's House dating from about 1780. There were once lots of wharfs along this side of the harbour, and just past the RNLI shop is a **black crane**, typical of many that used to be here.

Walk on past the Sailing Club, Lifeboat Station and Rowing Club towards the Stone Pier. Notice the **steps** going straight up to Nothe Gardens; the railway line balustrades were put in place to transport ammunition to and from Nothe Fort to boats serving the breakwater forts.

Pause at the **Stone Pier Café**. There has been a kiosk here since 1926 and it is an ideal place to watch boats coming and going. Vera makes homemade cakes on the premises and cooks to order, with daily specials. She has created an exhibition space for local artists, and helpfully sells everything needed for crabbing and basic fishing with the kids, as the end of the pier is a popular spot for this.

Just beyond the café, beside the old pill box, are some steps that lead down to a small, normally quiet, **stony beach**. The flint and chert pebbles here are fairly resistant to wave erosion and break up slowly compared to other local rocks. (See photograph at the beginning of the book.)

A The window has been blocked up to avoid paying Window Tax – from which we get the phrase 'daylight robbery'. Also notice the old Tudor-style wall in the dividing alley.

Q Near the start of the Pier, find the plaque telling the story of the *Earl of Abergavenny*.

Ill-fated Vessel! – ghastly shock!
At length delivered from the rock,
The deep she hath regained;
And through the stormy night they steer;
Labouring for life, in hope and fear,
To reach a safer shore – how near,
Yet not to be attained!

from *To the Daisy*, William Wordsworth

Go back to the café and take the steep path or steps up to Nothe Gardens and the Fort. Henry VIII, threatened with invasion by Spain and France following his to-do with the Pope, built a chain of artillery forts along the south coast, including the twin castles of Portland and Sandsfoot. A battery of guns would have been placed on the grassy ramparts at the Nose (the Nothe). During Elizabeth I's reign the fort was strengthened and became known as Queen Elizabeth's Fort. Much later a more permanent fort was built, construction commencing in 1860. The present fort took 12 years to build as the initial contractors pulled out, leaving the Royal Engineers and inmates of Portland Prison to finish it. It was used to house huge guns and supplies of ammunition and in the 19th century up to 400 men formed the garrison. Cannonballs have been found in the sea, probably practice shot. The entrance was originally over a drawbridge.

A In 1805 the ship ran aground on the Shambles near Portland Bill and ripped open her hull below the waterline. She desperately tried to reach Weymouth Sands but sank several miles offshore, with the loss of many lives including that of her captain, John Wordsworth, the brother of famous poet William Wordsworth, who penned *To the Daisy* (1805) as a heart-felt ode. A verse appears on the plaque.

The fort was strategically important during WWI when merchant and Royal Navy ships stationed in Portland Harbour were under attack from the Germans. Also, with air-raids on Weymouth's torpedo factories during WWII, search-lights and anti-aircraft guns were installed to help Dorset's only fighter squadron at RAF Warmwell defend our skies. By 1956 Portland Harbour was no longer a naval port so the fort was disbanded and fell into disuse, becoming a home for vagrants, until in the 1970s a group of volunteers transformed it into a museum and tourist attraction. With more than 70 rooms on three levels, it needs a full day to explore it all:

- Ramparts – from where the fort was originally defended with muskets and light muzzle-loaded cannons, now a good place to picnic while enjoying far-reaching views. During WWII, its guns could fire up to 20 shells per minute; hoists were used to carry cartridges from the basement magazines up to the guns.
- Ground floor and parade ground – 26 vaulted rooms provide a single semicircular gun deck approx. 150 m long. Visit the Barrack Room to see how crews lived alongside their guns, with their quota of 'official wives' helping with the laundry and cleaning. Their cannons could fire shells 3 miles (4.8 km) out to sea.
- Basement magazines – the long passages, tunnels and rooms were used as magazines for ammunition and stores, and now have lots of interesting

Q What are the shifting lobbies?

A The magazines (rooms) used to store gun powder and shells. Any spark or naked flame could set off a devastating explosion, so the soldiers had to change out of their uniforms, leaving their studded boots, belts and other metal objects in the 'shifting lobbies'.

displays. Children can do a treasure hunt for strategically placed mice in the maze of tunnels.

Each year over 3000 school children come from as far as Weston-super-Mare, as well as local Cubs, Scouts, Brownies and Guides, to experience life as an evacuee and learn about WWII as part of their curriculum. They can dress up, write a postcard home in the School Room, role play in the Laundry and Kitchen, get wet with the stirrup pump and hosepipe (with 'Sir' sneakily refilling the buckets), squeeze into an Anderson Shelter, and visit the Shop to decide what to buy with their old money and ration cards. The fort is also used as a corporate and private venue, for military festivals, concerts, rallies and theatre throughout the year. Live cannon and musket displays and arms drills are held once a fortnight on Sundays and during special events. If you fancy helping run the fort or firing a gun on the Parade Ground as an artillery volunteer, sign up in the Guard Room on the way out.

Walk back down Barrack Road past the Coastguard Cottages to Nothe Tavern. This inn was first leased to Eldridge Pope in 1877 and the Bullock family ran it for many years. Arthur Henry Bullock was a veteran of the Boer and Great Wars who lost both legs in 1945 yet continued to serve behind the bar in a wheelchair. It's a good family pub, with a small draughts table, games and books in a basket, newspapers and an eclectic mix of wall pictures and ceiling hangings.

Next to the Tavern is the **Friends Burial Ground**. This once overgrown plot has been transformed into a multi-faith community garden by the Weymouth Quaker Group and a team of volunteers including local garden designer and Chelsea Flower Show award-winner Michelle Brown. Chris Wilson, chairwoman of the project, said: 'We want to show that people of

different ages, beliefs, cultures, body shapes and faiths are great people, and as such we want to live in peace, celebrate peace and practise peace.' Representatives from other denominations including Holy Trinity Church, Weymouth Buddhist Group, the Jewish faith and Bournemouth Islamic Centre are involved, though people of no faith also support the project (email weymouthpeacegarden@hotmail.co.uk if you are interested). The gravestone of a little girl who was on the *Earl of Abergavenny* lies somewhere here. The garden also has a small turf maze, something quite rare now. People are encouraged to explore the garden and sit by the peace pole, enjoying the contemplative atmosphere of this inspired creation.

Feeling enriched, continue past **Wellington Court**, formerly the Red Barracks. This served as a cavalry barracks during the Napoleonic War, when troops from Hanover were stationed here. The sad story of two homesick Hussars is recounted in the 'Folklore' section of this book. Later the Red Barracks, one of three town barracks (others were situated in Coneygar Lane and on Lodmoor Hill), accommodated infantrymen; they are now private housing. Opposite are the Sea Cadets and Army/TA premises.

Q What building is next door to the former Red Barracks?

The Centre for Environment, Fisheries and Aquaculture (**CEFAS**) building opposite houses a fish laboratory, where they study fish diseases and toxins in the water.

Q What is engraved on the two entrance pillars?

Just past here is an alley called the **Lookout**. 'Throughout our history, men of Weymouth alerted to possible danger by sea-borne invaders, climbed from the snug streets of the old town and gazed out into the Channel from the "Lookout"' (Ricketts 1975, p.78).

Carry on down **Horsford St**, past the new brick houses which were awarded a Civic Society Certificate of Merit for being built in sympathy with the rest of the street. Turn right into **Spring Road** to return to Hope Square.

A The names of fish species and the diseases they are prone to.

A The old Military Arms public house, conveniently situated for the soldiers.

Walk 5: Castle, Cove and Trail

Start: Old Castle Road beach
Approx. distance: 5.5 km (including Nothe Gardens and Rodwell Trail). You could cycle this route or shorten it by treating it as a linear walk from Castle Cove to Spring Road (approx. 2 km).

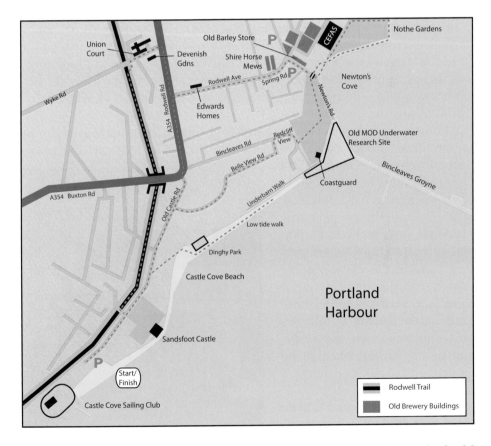

Castle Cove Sailing Club has its premises on the **beach at the end of Old Castle Road**. At low tide it is possible to follow the shoreline, skirting behind Sandsfoot Castle. Alternatively, walk up Old Castle Road to **Sandsfoot Gardens**.

In 1539 Henry VIII ordered the building of Sandsfoot and Portland Castles to challenge any ships attempting to sneak into Weymouth Harbour. Guns of Sandsfoot crossed the firing lines of Portland less than 2 miles (3.2 km) away, and they were probably built to a similar design; however, in reality neither castle saw any action against foreign forces, although Sandsfoot was used as a mint during the Civil War.

Almost as soon as it was built, **Sandsfoot Castle** (aptly named) began to topple. From 1665 it was considered unfit for use and left to decay, until today only a lovely ruin remains. With Heritage Lottery funding, the old castle has been given a new lease of life, with lighting, a walkway inside the walls and stabilisation of the structure, enabling visitors to go inside the castle for the first time in decades. Friends of Sandsfoot Castle and Rodwell Trail are developing a children's quiz and guides to the castle, and Tudor picnics are held in the gardens.

In the 1950s part of the gun deck of Sandsfoot Castle fell onto the beach below.

Next along the coast is **Castle Cove Beach** (known to locals as Sandsfoot Castle Beach). The shallow water here is good for a paddle. It is possible to walk along the beach as far as the concrete promontory, but then you will have to turn back as the cliffs here are only suitable for scaling by 'mountain goats'. The terrain and geology change along the way; in places the bottom layer of grey rock is densely packed with sea shells. The crumbling sandstone above is only really held together by vegetation, with trees growing right down to the beach, barely hanging on. Weathered hulks lie where they have lost root and tumbled, and water trickles out, further undermining the soft cliffs.

> **Q** Can you guess what the ramp and steps are used for?

Take the wooden steps back up to Old Castle Road and continue walking north. Turn right into **Belle Vue Road**, which has some lovely houses to admire.

Turn next right into **Redcliff View** (a no-through road) and pause at the green. To the right of the Coastguard is the old cliff path (Underbarn Walk) which is sadly falling away so that it is not possible to wander far along it now. This grassy area is a designated dog exercise place so feel free to release the hounds. Enjoy long-distance views of the Ridgeway, White Horse at Osmington and Hardy Monument as you **head across the green towards the Nothe**.

A The Sailing Club owned a building on the road above and built the ramp with steps down the middle specially to trail dinghies down to the sea.

Q Notice the metal ring set in concrete (of unknown origin) in the grass. What date is engraved on it?

As you drop down the hill, off to your right is **Bincleaves Groyne**. The old MoD underwater research establishment closed and was bought by QinetiQ, which paid for the redevelopment of this area including the new footbridge and attractive stonework. The grassy rocks fronting the shore are a quiet place to sit and admire **Newton's Cove**. Some steps nearby lead straight into the sea if you fancy a swim. The wall here was completed in 2003 and is made of blocks of Portland stone. Look carefully at blocks near the ice-cream kiosk and you may see fossilised shells within the limestone. The shells stand out because they are slightly more resistant to weathering. Bivalves (oysters and scallops) are particularly evident.

Q Just past the kiosk at the bottom of the wide steps, how can you tell your direction?

You may like to **wander along the prom** which is popular with local anglers, past the block building that houses the water inlet feed for the CEFAS laboratory above.

Q The carvings that decorate the wall here were produced at Weymouth College to celebrate some of the plants and creatures that lived in Jurassic times. What can you spot?

A Shells, squid, dragonfly, sea serpents, dinosaurs, ammonites, dog shark, coral, starfish and leaves.

A Use the compass set in the concrete.

A 1889.

An information board by the steps into the sea describes what flora and fauna to look out for along the shoreline today. The ledges are formed of calcareous sandstone. Lines of weakness in the sandstone have been weathered out to form vertical cracks, while acidic rainfall has selectively dissolved the calcium, giving the ledge a distinctive honeycomb appearance. The burrows of organisms that once lived in the sediment of the sea floor are also evident. The prom here was rebuilt in 1987 after a major landslip occurred, caused by the Nothe Clay above slumping during wet weather.

Loop up and round to the top path, returning to the footbridge. Drop down the steps below the bridge and turn right along Newton's Road. Go past the half-boarded building called the **Old Barley Store**. At the road junction, head left up **Spring Road**.

Q Devenish & Company's old Shire Horse Mews are immediately on your right. Name some of the brewery horses that used to live here.

From here, harbour and town are only a short distance away.

If you intend returning to the start of the walk/cycle, continue up Spring Road, which becomes Rodwell Avenue.

Q Nearing the top of the hill you pass an attractive row of houses known as Edwards Homes. When were these built?

A They were erected in 1896 by Sir Henry Edwards (MP and town benefactor) as homes for the elderly.

A Hector, Rupert, Goliath.

At the top of the road you could turn west onto Rodwell Road and take Old Castle Road straight back to Sandsfoot (the quickest route back). Or return along the Rodwell Trail – in which case turn right and after 200 m go left onto Wyke Road.

> **Q** Devenish Gardens on the left were the former residence of which Justice of the Peace?

Union Court apartments on the right used to be the old Portwey Hospital and before that the Union Workhouse.

Rodwell Trail passes under the road and the tunnel here was built to a design by Brunel (British civil engineer 1806–59). **Drop down onto the Trail and turn left. Follow it past Sandsfoot Castle Halt and then take the next left off the Trail back onto Old Castle Road.**

A Major John Herbert Clark Devenish.

Walk 6: Around Boot Hill

Start: Rodwell Road at the end of High West St (free parking in streets beyond Asda)
Finish: Old Town Hall
Approx. distance: 1.5 km

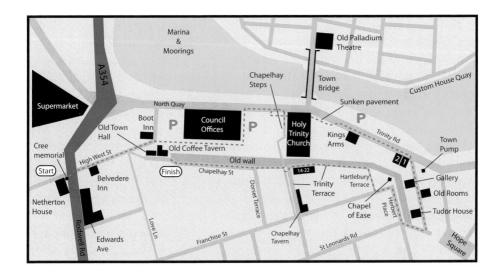

Stand on Rodwell Road just up from Asda by Netherton House with the traffic lights and crossing in front of you. Notice the **stone memorial** (by the railing behind you) to town benefactor John Cree from Osmington, who paid for the road widening here. Across the road is a row of ten cottages called

Edwards Avenue. These were built in 1894 and paid for by town benefactor and MP Sir Henry Edwards. His charity still helps local elderly people today who have difficulty financing and supporting themselves in their own homes.

Cross the road to High West St, the original high street of Weymouth. **Walk past the terraced cottages**, one of which is **Belvedere Inn** which replaced an earlier cottage. **At the end of this terrace is Love Lane**, 'a remarkable remnant of the Mediaeval street pattern' (Ricketts 1975), which would have seen much military action with troops heading for the **Old Town Hall on Boot Hill on the High Street in front of you**. This lovely old building was once the centre of Weymouth and seat of local government, with courts held here before the 1571 Charter. During the Civil War it was a central command post. In later centuries parts of the building were used as stables, a storehouse, prison, school, polling station and Girl Guide/Brownie meeting room. It was saved by a group of local people known as Guardians of the Old Town Hall who are turning it into a community centre, showcasing local art and culture.

The Boot Inn is a dog-friendly, old-style, drinkers' pub offering real ales and Cheddar Valley cider, and regular live music. In earlier times it was accessible from the harbourside and visitors to the inn could haul their boats up a slipway, which survives as the small road to the right of the building. The interior of the pub is dark and cosy, with original beams and an old 'floating peat floor' cellar, ideal for keeping barrels of ale cool. It is not sure how the *Boot* got its name. Possibly it comes from an old tannery and cobblers shop that stood on the site of the nearby Municipal Building, or from the old wooden boot sign that commonly graced inn frontages of this type before painted signs became commonplace; the boot indicated that travellers were welcome and they could enjoy a 'wash and brush up' here. Another story tells how a Revenue officer, who was making enquiries in the inn, was set upon, roughed up and 'booted' out of the pub. So take your pick. Inside is a collection of old boots and a picture entitled 'The Seven Stages of Man', depicting seven boots of various styles and sizes. On the wall is a spoon-shaped wooden oar inscribed with the words 'Ponty's Holy Batten' commemorating Ponty Groves, a fisherman and lifeboat man who frequented the inn and who was, according to the barman, 'the biggest s**t-stirrer in town' – hence the oar. The 'Rules of the Inn' by the Gents toilet is also a chuckle.

The old Weymouth Coffee Tavern opposite is now a Kingdom Hall of Jehovah's Witnesses. **Walk through the car park behind the council offices.** This was originally part of the High Street and it was here that a major historic battle was won. Outnumbered by at least 4:1, Parliamentarians stationed cannons on the **old wall above** and musketeers in the windows of the houses that once overlooked this. They lured and trapped 2500-odd Royalists into this tight area, where they were cut to ribbons; it was said that the blood flowed down the street and turned the river red for two nights. Years later, shouts and screams have been heard here. The bank is laced with tunnels. During the 14th/15th century, Weymouth was a big importer of ice, and according to George Ellis (*Histories and Antiquities of Old Weymouth*, 1829) there is an old ice cavern in the back wall of the Old Town Hall.

At the end of the council building, turn left before the 'Visitors' car park, then right along Trinity Road, a continuation of the old High Street. **Pause at Chapelhay Steps by the church to look at the Town Bridge**. A first bridge was built here in 1597 in an attempt to bring together the squabbling communities of Weymouth and Melcombe Regis. It had 17 arches and a drawbridge and needed 30 great oak trees to construct it. It was damaged during the Civil War, the drawbridge constantly going up and down against the raiders, and was rebuilt later in 1713 and 1741. At the time of Judge Jeffery, a gallows was erected at Greenhill and heads and quarters were displayed on the bridge to dampen the spirit of further rebels. Hung, drawn and quartered remains were disposed of around the borough as follows:

1 quarter and 2 heads at Town Bridge
1 quarter and 2 heads at Melcombe Town Hall
2 quarters at Weymouth Town Hall
4 quarters and 1 head near the windmill
2 quarters at Weymouth town end
6 quarters and 1 head at the grand pier

Beyond the bridge on the opposite side of the river is Custom House Quay. In 1769 the number of ships moored at the Quay was so great that cargoes required hoisting over several vessels. So it was decided to build a new bridge slightly further up river in line with the Sailors Return in order to lengthen the Quay. However, by 1821, following debate about the advantages of this new site, the old bridge was taken down and replaced by a new stone bridge with a swing section on the previous old site. The present bridge was built in 1930. There was talk of welding it shut, but thanks to a High Court case instigated by Barry Curtis, who campaigned for the rights of boat owners to go into the inner harbour, it has remained a lifting bridge.

The **large building at the end of the bridge** on the right was constructed pre-1900. It was originally a furniture showroom for Messrs Hawkes Freeman, then became a cinema, the Palladium Theatre. This closed shortly after the 'Talkies' arrived, with *Port of Lost Souls* and *Life's Like That* the last films shown (rather apt titles). During WWII the building was used as a Services club, after which it became a motorcycle showroom with workshops in the basement run by Pankhurst well into the 1960s. It was then converted into a nightclub.

Holy Trinity Church overlooking the Bridge is '... an inventive and remarkable solution on a most difficult site. The enormous slope from south to north and the raised approach of the 1824 bridge were turned to good account. A large crypt was formed with an entry from the High Street passage passing below the elevated entrance and steps. The main body of the church thus dominates the street and harbour scene' (Ricketts 1975, p.109). It was later extended by local architect G.R. Crickmay in 1886. Its impressive interior contains marble mural tablets by local sculptor Isaac Hellyer.

Backtrack slightly and take the steps down to the sunken pavement, which in Tudor times was level with the old road. Half way along the covered section a door leads into the catacombs. Further on, notice how some of the doorsteps are raised; this is because at high tide the pavement could flood.

The **Kings Arms** is an old pub (16th century) with attics added later in the 19th century.

> **Q** Outside is a collecting vessel for the RNLI. What is unusual about this?

In 1918 a German submarine surfaced and surrendered in Weymouth Bay, and another did the same in 1945; the submarine was photographed

A It is an old German mine, found in Weymouth Bay in 1948.

in the harbour here, just in front of No. 1 Harbour House further down the road.

No. 2 is Ralph Allen's former residence. Allen was a quarry owner, the Mayor of Bath and an important socialite in King George's day, who made his fortune by reorganising the postal system. In 1750 he came to Weymouth on the advice of his doctors and was so enamoured by the place he bought a summer residence here. He encouraged the Prince of Wales (who later became George III) to visit the town, and the rest is history.

The **Town Pump** used to be sited on North Quay until 1990 when it was relocated here. The stocks too were moved here in the early 1700s from their original position outside the Old Town Hall. 'Criminals' endured the taunts and rotten food thrown by passers-by for crimes such as playing the fiddle whilst drunk on a Sunday and for swearing oaths.

Round the corner in Trinity St is Leighton Art Gallery. This old brewery building used to be a sugar store, then became a sail loft and is now an art and antiques centre, with a painting gallery and studio offering art classes.

The Old Rooms on the left side of the road are believed to have been the home of merchant and Mayor Thomas Giear. In 1618 he was found guilty of defrauding the King (by pocketing the various duties paid by foreign ships for wharf, ballast, drawing, bridge lifting and cargo) and was fined the colossal sum of £2000. The Old Rooms became a summer boarding house and the Duke of Gloucester stayed here. During the Napoleonic Wars it was an inn, reputed to be frequented by press gangs. Thomas Hardy wrote a tale called *A Committee-Man of the Terror*, in which one of the characters stayed at The Old Rooms Inn, and the hostelry also features in his novel *The Dynasts*. In Georgian times it was extended and became an entertainment venue, the Assembly Rooms, where people met to discuss matters of the day and enjoy entertainment. It was the place to see and be seen.

A little further down the street is Tudor House, originally a rich merchant's dwelling.

> **Q** Study the front of this building. What suggests it might once have been two separate homes?

Wind round to the right and up St Leonards Rd. Bear right into Herbert Place. In the corner of a private garden at the far end of the residents parking area can just be seen a small (Listed) chapel of ease. Pilgrims would have paid their respects here before sailing to Spain.

Continue round the corner into Franchise St. This is well named as it used to house several traders and numerous public houses, the only one surviving today being Chapelhay Tavern. Between these two streets an aerial mine landed in 1940, damaging 879 houses and killing 12 people. After that the area was demolished and rebuilt.

Turn right along Hartlebury Terrace, then left into Trinity Terrace. Several cats frequent this area. Be sure to pause for views of the town and discreetly admire the pretty houses and gardens here.

> **Q** What is carved on the keystones above the doors of Nos 14–22?

At the end of the Terrace, descend the steps to the right, turn left up the hill and take the flight of steps up to Chapelhay St, one of the oldest streets in Weymouth. Prior to 1872 it was called St Nicholas Street as it led to Weymouth's first chapel, dedicated to St Nicholas, patron saint of travellers. French raiders targeted the town on Sundays and Feast Days when most townsfolk were worshipping a mile or so away at their nearest church, All

 A series of heads, as elsewhere around the town.

 The twin gables and walled-up door on the right. Also, picture this house on the edge of a water inlet. Rain water in the guttering would have flowed straight off the roof into the harbour.

Saints in Wyke, so to combat this problem they built St Nicholas chapel. It was used as a fort during the Civil War, when it received a battering. In 1853 it was cleared to make way for a new school; this was demolished after bomb damage and today houses stand on the old chapel site, which aligns with the rest of St Nicholas Street across the river (to the right of the Sailors Return). In medieval times the harbour at this point was crossable by rope ferry.

Walk along the top of the old wall. This was a strategic spot, affording views of the whole town, backwater, sea and Wyke. Major Francis Sydenham, commander of the Parliamentarians, was allegedly shot in the head coming up the steps just behind this wall. Cannons here would have been trained upon the old bridge below. There were rumoured to be tunnels running from the Town Hall to St Nicholas chapel, and also to the catacombs of Holy Trinity Church at the bottom of the hill. Priests may have used these tunnels to move secretly between buildings.

> **Q** Just before the Old Town Hall there is a brick wall. What can you see disappearing into the wall?

You are now back at the Old Town Hall.

 Steps here are all that remain of one of the houses that used to overlook the Back Water. A former occupant remembers the tunnels under this house, which, upon investigation, were found to run all the way to Sandsfoot Castle. When the Armada was caught in the tides of the Race and blown to pieces, Spanish vessels were towed back into the harbour. Instead of stone, they had ballast of gold and silver on board (as payment for the Spanish military). It is suspected that the Mayor of Weymouth looted some of the treasure, using the tunnels to fetch it secretly away to Sandsfoot.

Other Walks and Cycling Routes

Active Travel. Weymouth & Portland: A Guide to Walking and Cycling is available from the TIC or can be downloaded from www.dorsetforyou.com/activetravelmaps and will help with planning a route. Also the leaflet *Parklife* details four circular walks through Weymouth's parks and gardens, varying in length from 1.5 to 8 miles (2.4–12.9 km). The Seaside Saunter, Heritage Trail and Round Ramble start at the small car park at Nothe Gardens, the Willow Walk from Princess of Wales Gardens.

Wey Valley Walks

The River Wey begins life as a spring bubbling out of Windsbatch Hill, surfacing at Upwey at the Wishing Well. It meanders for 4.5 miles (7.3 km), initially as a small brook, through fields and villages, dispensing its short self into Weymouth Harbour. A series of footpaths following the river extend from Radipole Lake into the AONB as far as Ridgeway Hill, where it is possible to link with other trails.

The Wey Valley waymarked route is split into six coloured walks of varying length, the longest being 6.5 miles (10.5 km) and the shortest 4.5 miles (7.3 km). Information leaflets are currently out of print, so use an Ordnance Survey map to guide you. The longest route begins at the RSPB Centre at Radipole Lake, goes through housing and on to Radipole village, where it passes through Humpty Dumpty Field, the site of the medieval village just west of St Ann's Church.

As the path leaves old Radipole, there is a small stone bridge opposite Letterbox Cottage. A stone in the river here has special significance. Over the centuries, a 'Beating the Bounds' ceremony was held, traditionally during the fifth week after Easter, when people would walk the 10–12 miles (16–19.3 km). around the borough's boundaries. On the way they would bless the crops and give thanks to God. These boundaries were marked by stones, gates, walls and trees, and in the old days boys and girls were 'bumped' or sometimes beaten with a rod at these boundary posts 'to determine and preserve recollection of its extent, and to see that no encroachments have been made upon it, and that the landmarks have not been taken away' (William Barnes, quoted in Udal 1989). Weymouth Museum has the original ebony and silver boundary rods. The long but jolly walk also involved rowing boats and the scaling of walls. Nowadays, the Mayor and Corporation occasionally re-enact the ceremony, with school children carrying small boundary rods.

Along the River Wey are a series of watermills, the majority now converted into houses. Nottington has an old mill and malthouse. The Spa House used to house baths, a pump room and a sulphurous spring. The Wey Valley Walk proceeds to Broadwey, then along the road to Upwey and Westbrook House (dated 1620). In the village is a stone mill built in 1802, one of the largest in England at 7×3 m (22×9 ft). The spring water at the Wishing Well is naturally clear and the well is said to produce 6.8 million litres (1.5 million gallons) of water a day and never dries up.

Approaching Upwey, a branch of the Wey Valley Walks splits off west to Hewish Farm, Windsbatch, Friar Waddon and up onto Ridgeway Hill, through Winterbourne Abbas and across fields back into Upwey. Another route goes east to Bincombe and the Iron Age hillfort of Chalbury; the main enclosure covers 8.5 acres (3.4 ha) and shows signs of extensive occupation, with terraces on the north side (strip lynchets) constructed in the Middle Ages to make ploughing possible. The route proceeds round the back of Came Wood and returns to Bincombe.

Rodwell Trail

A railway was built in 1865 to carry passengers and stone between Weymouth and Portland. It was extended into the Royal Navy Dockyards in 1878 and later in 1891 served Whitehead's torpedo factory at Ferrybridge, which had its own siding and pier with narrow-gauge track out into Portland Harbour. The line closed in 1965 and the track was taken up and tarmac laid to made a smooth surface for pedestrians and cyclists – known as the Rodwell Trail. The Trail officially runs from the Chesil Beach Centre to Abbotsbury Road

Rodwell Trail provides a green artery through town, with great views, the Trail often level with the rooftops of houses. It has atmospheric wooded parts along the way; be sure to whistle as you go through the tunnels.

near Westham Bridge and it is a pleasant walk or cycle along its 2.5 miles (3.4 km) of car-free, level track. The pillars at the Abbotsbury Road end used to guard the entrance to the old naval accommodation on Portland. Along the way, you pass information boards, old railway halts and an anti-aircraft gun emplacement. Sandsfoot Castle is accessible from the route. At Ferrybridge the Trail continues as pavement across the Bridge, then joins the old railway line across common land alongside Portland Harbour. This is a sea of pink thrift flowers from April. Near the end of Portland Beach Road the Trail follows a permissive route through Osprey Quay to Portland Castle.

Cycling

Weymouth boasts 28 km of existing traffic-free cycle routes; these link the main residential areas, and future routes are planned to connect with new housing developments, to encourage cycling rather than car use.

- The 6.5-km *Rodwell Trail and Portland Beach Road* route links Weymouth town centre to Portland, starting at Westham Bridge and progressing to Victoria Square in Fortuneswell. The route follows the old railway line and is a sealed surface with gentle gradient throughout. Further sections will follow as funding becomes available.
- The sealed surface, 1-km *Osprey Quay* route forms a spur off the Portland Beach Road route, taking in the National Sailing Academy.
- The 2.25-km *Granby Way* and 1.25-km *Radipole Lake* cycle routes provide traffic-free connections between Granby Industrial Estate, Chickerell and the town centre.
- The 2.25-km *National Cycle Network route 26* links the town centre and Swannery with Radipole via Radipole Park Drive and then follows the 8.5 km of traffic-free cycle route between Manor Roundabout and Stadium Roundabout in Dorchester as part of the Weymouth Relief Road.
- The 5-km *Redlands and Preston Beach Road* cycle routes link Preston, Lodmoor and the Mount Pleasant park-and-ride site.
- The 1.6-km *Marsh Route (phase 1)* links Westham and Lanehouse Rocks Road with the Rodwell Trail and town centre.

A number of further cycle routes are planned including:

- The 2-km *Marsh Route (phase 2)* linking Budmouth College, the swimming pool, outdoor education centre and athletics track with Chickerell.
- The 2-km *Littlemoor* route being built as part of the Weymouth Relief Road.
- The *Eastern Route* which will link Radipole Park Drive with Preston Beach Road, to join the cycleway from the Sealife Centre along Preston promenade to Overcombe.

The website www.dorsetforyou.com/weymouthtransportschemes has up-to-date information on progress with the various routes. Adam Bows, Principal Transport Planner at Dorset County Council, explains:

'Weymouth is a key priority for promoting cycling because of the dispersed nature of housing and destinations. For instance, from Southill it's a 30-minute walk to the town centre, which is too far for many people, but by bike it only takes about 10 minutes. There is great potential for linking existing cycle routes and improving others. We are building on the investment in the Relief Road, the Weymouth Transport Package and Connect 2 (the new bridge at Newstead Road) to fund expansion of the local cycle network.

There are a couple of tricky areas. We'd like to widen the cycle path along Portland Beach Road, but owing to the unique habitat (it's a Special Area of Conservation, which is the highest level of international protection) it's not possible to build into the shingle. This means we have to widen into the carriageway, which will be costly. The other difficult area is along the Esplanade where cycling is prohibited. Both Weymouth and Portland Borough Council and DCC would like to allow cycling outside high season and at off-peak times, as at Bournemouth, but this requires amendment of the existing bylaw. This is a problem because the bylaw also affects street peddling – it restricts anyone setting up a stall along the seafront unless they obtain a licence. If the bylaw was rescinded to help cyclists, it would mean the council would lose its power over street peddlers. So, despite a survey in which the majority of local people said they would be happy to allow responsible cycling along the prom, the ban looks set to continue.'

Local cyclists Anne and Ken Neale have compiled a useful resource of information –www.akweb.org.uk/weyroute – including 12 detailed local cycle routes, which you can print out and/or download for your GPS, mapping software and Google Earth.

CTC Wessex (www.wessexctc.org/) organises events and local rides of varying pace and style. They also arrange visits to France and have a long-standing twinning agreement with the Union Cyclotourism de Saint Lô to enjoy exchange visits. The group also campaigns for cycling facilities; see http://www.akweb.org.uk/strategy.html for their comments in response to the Weymouth and Portland Cycling and Walking Strategy.

Cycle West (http://cycle-west.com/index.php) promotes cycle tourism on both sides of the Channel. Seventeen partners have signed up to the initiative including the counties of Dorset, Devon and Cornwall, French regions Normandy and Brittany, and shipping lines Brittany Ferries and Condor Ferries. The project is funding 1100 miles (1771 km) of new cycle routes to link scenic countryside and tourist attractions in those areas. Three major itineraries are offered. The Petit Tour de Manche takes in Weymouth, a circular route of 248 miles (400 km) between St Malo, Mont Saint-Michel, Cherbourg, Poole, Weymouth and Jersey.

Help and Information

Maps

The general area is covered by OS Explorer Map OL15 and Landranger 194. A detailed map of the town is available from the TIC.

Transport

Buses to Portland leave from Town Bridge and North Quay (near the Council offices). Services to Dorchester, Abbotsbury and Bridport depart from the King's Statue. A double-decker bus (Coastlink X53) passes through Weymouth, hugging the World Heritage Coast on its journey between Poole and Exeter. Trains leave from the railway station in King St for London twice hourly and for Bristol several times a day.

Tourist Information Centre

Pavilion Theatre, The Esplanade, Tel 01305 785747, email: tic@weymouth.gov. uk, www.visitweymouth.co.uk. Open 7 days a week: 9.30 am–5 pm April to October, 9.30 am–4 pm November to March

Weymouth Museum

Brewers Quay, www.weymouthmuseum.org.uk. (note: at the time of printing, the Museum has relocated while Brewers Quay is being developed)

The Museum houses the Borough Collection and offers talks and exhibitions throughout the year. The Local History Unit looks after the Museum's collection of postcards, photos, posters, maps, pamphlets, electoral registers and other reference material. It also holds microfilm copies of some borough archives dating from the 14th century. Access is by appointment.

Weymouth Library

Great George St, Tel 01305 762410, www.dorsetforyou.com/libraries

Weymouth Library is a fine example of what a library should be, with excellent facilities, a light and airy atmosphere, encouraging children's section and extra room upstairs for quiet reading, study and meetings. Facilities include:

- Hire of CD-ROMs, language courses, music and drama sets (play reading, performance sets).
- Home library service: volunteers deliver to housebound people including care homes.
- Rhyme Time: singing and stories for babies to pre-schoolers.
- Events: including family history drop-ins.
- Reading groups: two groups meet in the library, others privately.
- Read Easy: volunteers help adults who have difficulty reading.
- Off the Page: a poetry project aimed at 16–25 year olds.
- My Voice: a performance-based project for 11–19 year olds.
- Bag Books: interactive reading sessions for adults with severe learning difficulties.
- Friends of Weymouth Library: talks, coffee mornings, trips and themed evenings.
- Story-time: with craft activities during school holidays.

Beach Office and Lifeguards

The Beach Office on the Esplanade manages the beach and operates from the only building on the prom, adjacent to the King's Statue. It acts as a point of call for missing people including lost children, first-aid, advice on bylaws and other uses of the beach. RNLI lifeguards are based near here and operate during the summer from 10 am to 6 pm.

Useful Contacts and Sources of Information

www.weymouth.gov.uk
www.waterfrontweymouth.co.uk
www.weymouth-dorset.co.uk
www.visit-weymouth.tv
Tourist Information Centre – 01305 785747, www.visitweymouth.co.uk
Harbour Masters Office – 01305 838423, www.harbour.weymouth.gov.uk
Weymouth Marina – 01305 767576, VHF Channel 80
Coastwatch – 01305 860178
Beach Office – 01305 838511
Lifeguards – 01305 767188
Royal Dorset Yacht Club – 01305 786258, www.royal-dorset.com
T.S. Pelican – 01305 839476, www.adventureundersail.com

Condor Ferries – 0845 6091026, www.condorferries.com
Fleet Observer – 01305 759692
Chesil Beach Centre – 01305 760579, www.chesilbeach.org
Nothe Fort – 01305 766626, www.nothefort.org.uk
Weymouth Angling Centre – 01305 785032

Bibliography

Attwooll M (2001) *Weymouth: The Golden Years*. Dorset Books, Tiverton.

Attwooll M, Pomeroy CA (2004) *Weymouth Revisited*. Dorset Books, Tiverton.

Attwooll M (2009) *Second Bumper Book of Weymouth*. Dorset Books, Wellington.

Bellamy J (2006) *101 Churches in Dorset*. SB Publications, Seaford.

Boddy M, West J (1983) *Weymouth: An Illustrated History*. Dovecote Press, Wimborne.

Brodie A, *et al*. (2008) *Weymouth's Seaside Heritage*. English Heritage, Swindon.

Bruce P (2001) *Inshore Along the Dorset Coast*. Boldre Marine, Lymington.

Crowden J, Wright R, Wright G (2007) *Dorset Coast*. Flagon Press, Ilminster.

Dwyer J (2009) *Dorset Pioneers*. The History Press, Stroud.

Gutteridge R (1984) *Dorset Smugglers*. Dorset Publishing Co., Sherborne.

Holiday A (undated) *A Geological Walk Around Weymouth*.www. dorsetgeologistsassociation.com

Hutchins' History of Dorset Vol II. Available in Dorset Records Office, Dorchester.

Kelly's Directory of Dorsetshire 1898. Available in Dorset Records Office, Dorchester.

Lucking JH (1971) *The Great Western at Weymouth*. David & Charles, Newton Abbot.

Newland RJ, North MJ (2007) *Dark Dorset*. CFZ Press, Bideford.

Oppitz L (2001) *Lost Railways of Dorset*. Countryside Books, Newbury.

Payne D (1953) *Dorset Harbours*. Christopher Johnson, London.

Pomeroy C (2005) *Wings Over Weymouth*. Dovecote Press, Wimborne.

Reeby M (1995) *Taking the Waters at Weymouth*. Spa Publications, Weymouth.

Ricketts E (1975) *The Buildings of Old Weymouth. Part One*. Lithopress, Weymouth.

Ricketts E (1976) *The Buildings of Old Weymouth. Part Two*. Lithopress, Weymouth.

Taylor, Christopher (undated) *The Making of the English Landscape: Dorset*. Available in Dorset Records Office, Dorchester.

Udal J Symonds (1989) *Dorsetshire Folk-Lore*. Dorset Books, Exeter.

Webb P (2007) *Weymouth's Narrow Gauge Torpedo Railways*. Paul Webb, Weymouth.

Westwood R (2008) *Historic Dorset*. Inspiring Places, Fordingbridge.

http://www.users.globalnet.co.uk/~wykedh/webgeorge/index.htm

Index